CHRISTMAS , AT LAST

A NOVEL BY:

BRIAN ZIROLI and Jacob

Contents

PROLOGUE

Do you believe in angels? Do you believe that a higher power appears through every day people?

Do you think that we simply are victims of our own choices? Or, do you think our lives are already pre-planned, and everything happens for a reason? Do you believe that everything must happen according to a plan that God has set up for each of us?

Have you ever taken time to really think about these things?

Times change. Situations change. For the most part, people do not change.

But, what does change is within a person's heart. The heart is extremely powerful.

When we open our hearts, there are literally endless possibilities. And perhaps God, through other people, or through angels, helps us open our hearts to a different way of thinking, a different way of feeling, a different way of learning...a different way of living. I know this for certain. I experienced it firsthand with my grandparents and parents.

Kristy

CHAPTER 1

"Jesus, how long does it take to get my chocolate sundae?"

"Hold your pants, Mr. Evans." "Don't get your diapers in a dander."

Jane Fremont knew how to dish it out. After all these years, she knew how to deal with the likes of Mr. Evans.

She hadn't been at Rosemont quite as long as James Evans had, but long enough. Rosemont had grown to house not only elderly in need of nursing care, but also rehabilitative services. More recently, it seemed like younger people, in their 60's, were coming to Rosemont for longer-term care. The majority of the residents, however were 75 and above.

Those who had been at Rosemont for over 10 years were considered "lifers". James Evans was a lifer. It wasn't that he was that old, really. He just acted old.

Three things were certain at Rosemont – breakfast, lunch and supper – 8:00 a.m., noon, and 5:00 p.m., respectively. James enjoyed a small chocolate sundae at supper, regardless of the dessert of the day.

"I get sexually aroused when you talk like that, Jane."

"Ha! I doubt you've been sexually aroused since the Reagan administration."

A low crescendo of laughter came from James' table. Laughter was more the exception than the rule. There were a few "rebels", and James was one of them.

Nothing new to report at this dinner time. Many older folks were half-asleep. Half of them had to be reminded to eat. The others thought the food wasn't being served quickly enough, and they let the staff know.

James sat with John Woodson, Alvin Mericade, and William Hersch. They weren't so much close friends, as they had been assigned to the table by the Rosemont administration. Every six months or so, some of the residents would have their seating changed. Rosemont believed this would encourage more camaraderie. It was a nice idea – in theory.

There were more women than men at Rosemont. Most reasoned that women live longer. It was probably 65%-35% in favor of the women. There was an assortment of ailments among the lifers – strokes, dementia, COPD, partial paralysis. Some required oxygen tanks.

Between meals, there was always a variety of activities for the residents. Wednesday nights were for the dogs. A few trained dogs came in. They always seemed to perform the same tricks. Tuesday and Thursday nights were for music and movie trivia. Saturday afternoons were reserved for Bingo. James always thought it was interesting that the bingo chips were the size of half dollars.

James finished his sundae, and it was time to head back to his room – D5 – Wing D, Room 5. He did not have to share a room with another resident. As a lifer, he had earned that benefit. Television was his best friend. As a sports fanatic, at least he had something to watch during the day. Ask any of the residents and they would tell you that the biggest challenge was not always their health. It was time. There may be 24 hours in a day, but for the residents, time stood still. For them, a day could feel like an eternity.

Emily Hahn helped James get back to his room. Emily was one of several aides. James could walk. He was not relegated to a wheelchair permanently, but he needed some assistance with washing and dressing. He often used a walker, but still needed help sometimes. Even if he could walk he probably wouldn't say. He liked the idea of young, pretty aides having to hold and touch him. He was old, but he wasn't dead.

Like many residents, after a meal, he was immediately taken to his bathroom. For James, it was one of several trips to the bathroom each day. He had problems with one of his kidneys. He knew they were starting to get worse, but he tried not to let on.

"Sweetie, as always, thanks for the ride," James said to Emily.

"You are very welcome. Now, let's get you on the pot." Emily always was pretty straightforward.

Having someone help you with getting on the toilet can be humbling to say the least. It was extremely difficult in the beginning, but over time, James seemed to accept the fact that he needed help. It still felt demeaning.

After being cleaned up by Emily, James used his walker to the main resident lobby. There was one big screen television. Reruns of "The Lawrence Welk Show" played every night. He'd seen them all. But, with no visitors or family, the nights could be extremely long.

There were plenty of times James preferred to stay in his room. If his beloved Boston Red Sox were on television, you couldn't drag him away. Sports were his family. He knew what to expect. He could depend on it.

"How ya doing, Mr. Evans?"

"Oh, same shit, different day," he said to Rosie Vaughn. Rosie was a big woman who was usually seen at the front entrance when visitors arrived. Quite frankly, she was lazy and unmotivated. She did more gabbing and gossiping than actually screening visitors. But she had been a fixture at Rosemont. She was intimidating, and no one was going to tell her how to do her job.

"I hear ya, "she replied.

"Working late tonight, Rosie?"

"On my way out now. You have yourself a good night, Mr. Evans."

"Good night, Rosie."

"Get yourself some sleep – big day tomorrow," she said as her voice tailed off.

After James was taken back to his room, he was cleaned up and helped into his pajamas. Then, as usual, he was given the option of sitting in his recliner, or going into his bed. On this night, he chose the bed. Amanda Verdutti was the nurse assigned to James on this night.

"How's that feel – want the pillow up more, Mr. Evans?"

"No, that's perfect, Amanda...just like you."

She laughed. "You're so full of shit. Where did you get that sense of humor?"

"It's on rental...till I die."

"That's cute. Well, you should have it a long time since you are going to be around for a while."

"That's what I'm afraid of," James said. "Hey, Rosie said it was a big day tomorrow. What's going on?"

"A big day?" Amanda asked. "I know we have a new resident arriving."

"Ah, shit, is that all? I thought maybe you were going to tell me Beyonce was coming."

"Beyonce? How do you know Beyonce?"

"Hey, I'm cultured – I watch TV. What's it going to be this time?"

"You mean male or female? I believe we have a lady arriving," Amanda noted.

James didn't seem surprised. "Swell, another dame. As if this place wasn't crawling with enough old ladies."

"You know you love it, Mr. Evans. Another lady to experience your charm and humor."

"Hmmm. More like another lady who'll watch her bank account go to Rosemont."

"See, there's that sense of humor she will experience."

"Ah, hell. Won't affect me none."

Actually, nothing would ever be the same for James Evans.

CHAPTER 2

A new resident was a big deal – at least that's what Rosemont wanted everyone to believe. They wanted to make the new person feel at home as quickly as possible. The idea was to make the new resident feel like everyone was his or her new friend – like it was their birthday and Christmas all in one. But, that feeling eventually wore off when they realized they were actually in a nursing home. And, in most cases, they were not going home.

It was a tradition at Rosemont that all new residents go through an "orientation." First, they met with one or two members of the executive management team who oversaw the entire orientation program. Next, they met the nurses, and aides, and the cafeteria staff, to make sure Rosemont had the person's health background and proper dietary summary. Then, the new resident and his/her family tried to stop by each room to say hello and meet the current residents. They were eventually shown to their new room, complete with balloons, streamers and the like.

At one point in time, Rosemont would line up all the residents in the entrance foyer. When a new resident arrived, they would all yell "surprise!" It was a nice gesture and it looked like it was going to be a long standing tradition. That is, until new resident Edward Masik arrived on his first day some years ago. It would end up being his last day on earth. It wasn't properly communicated to all the staff that Edward had been experiencing major heart problems. When everyone yelled "surprise", he went into cardiac arrest. Certainly Rosemont feared a legal battle with Edward's family. They didn't need to worry. There would be no lawsuit from the Edward Masik estate. Though it was never confirmed, Rosemont management had heard that the surviving children made out very well after the reading of Edward's will. The theory was that a dead Edward was worth a lot more to the survivors than paying a large monthly fee to Rosemont. Edward's children took their money and went their separate ways. Rosemont never heard from them again. Just to be safe though, Rosemont stopped the practice of "surprising" new residents.

CHAPTER 3

Mary Hubert arrived about 2:30 p.m. with her daughters, Jennifer and Jacqueline, and her son, Anthony. A couple of Rosemont's top brass greeted and welcomed Mary and her family. They were taken on a quick tour of the facility. The application process had been completed by Mary's daughters. Anthony did not stay in this western Pennsylvania town. He had moved to Boston several years prior. He was married to his wife, Lori. Jennifer was still single. "Jacqui" had been divorced for six years now. Her ex-husband lived in the Dallas/Forth Worth area.

With Anthony living in Boston, it had been pretty much left to Jennifer and Jacqui to find the right nursing home for Mary. They chose Rosemont because it had what they were looking for – a clean facility, a large staff, qualified nurses and aides -- and it had an opening. There were waiting lists at most of the good nursing homes in the surrounding area. If there was an opening available, you almost had to take it. In addition, Rosemont was fairly close to Jennifer and Jacqui, so they could visit often.

Mary was shown to her room. She would stay in Wing A temporarily. Typically, new residents were placed in a "transitional" room in Wing A for the first few months. Only when they got used to the everyday itinerary and activities of the facility would they then be moved to a permanent room in another wing.

Mary now needed some assistance with everyday activities. Her daughters did the best they could to keep her in her own house, but it was at the point where she needed more professional care. The family made the very difficult decision to put her in a nursing home.

After seeing where she would be staying, Mary was then taken on a tour to meet the other residents. During this time, her family was taken to a conference room to complete some more paperwork. Some of the residents were very talkative, while others usually did not say much more than a "hello." Most were cordial to new residents. They knew what they were in for.

When Mary came by James' room on her tour, he quickly noticed that she still had very distinguished features for her age. *She must have been awfully pretty when she was young,* James thought.

Jenna Rutherford introduced James to Mary. If Jenna was available, she was usually hand-picked to introduce the new residents. She had a very cheerful demeanor and personality, and had the ability to make the new residents feel at ease.

"Mary, this is James Evans. He has been at Rosemont for quite some time. I'm sure Mr. Evans would be more than helpful if you ever have any questions."

"Absolutely," James said. "In addition to being a resident, I own half this joint."

"Mary, you will also find Mr. Evans somewhat humorous and full of himself," Jenna noted.

"It's nice to meet you, sir**."** James noticed she had a quiet, almost youthful voice. He also noticed she had an ease about her. She looked straight into his eyes as if she was looking through him. He also noticed that she was very well dressed. Her hair color was varying shades of white and gray, and it looked like she had just been at a hairdresser.

"Are you from this area, Mary?"

"Well, I am originally from here. I have lived in a few places – my husband was in the military."

"Oh, is he here with you?"

"No, he passed on several years ago."

"I'm sorry to hear that."

James could sense sadness in Mary. Certainly there would be a flood of emotions with entering a nursing home for the first time, but it was more than that.

Jenna intervened. "Well, let's keep you moving, Mary."

"Nice meeting you again, sir."

"Nice meeting you. Good luck to you."

CHAPTER 4

5:00 sharp. Time for supper.

James observed that Mary was assigned to the table next to him. The staff located extra chairs for Jennifer, Jacqui, and Anthony. He wondered how long it would be before she would be eating by herself. That could be very difficult.

Because it was her first day at Rosemont, Mary was presented with a large cake, including candles. The staff brought out balloons and flowers. Her family seemed genuinely pleased and surprised. They all had overwhelmed looks on their faces, as all new residents' families do. It would take a while, but Mary would eventually learn that this would be her "new normal."

Jennifer, Jacqui, and a couple of aides took Mary outside after dinner to show her the large pond and gazebo. Rosemont liked to refer to the surrounding grounds as the "campus."

James saw Anthony pass by his room. "Your mom is outside with your sisters," James yelled out.

"Oh, yeah, I know. I was just looking around the place," replied Anthony.

"Come on in, if you want."

"Thank you." They shook hands and Anthony took a seat.

"Your mom seems like a real nice lady."

"Yeah, we're all a little nervous.   We just wanted to make sure this works for her.   She's had a lot of help from my sisters the past few years, but at least she was able to stay in her own house."

"It's a big change; I'm not going to lie. But she'll get used to it, and will fit right in," James said, trying to reassure him.

"I just wish I could stay longer, or lived closer. That's really bothering me."

"Oh, you live out of town?"

"I live in Boston. I work in financial management."

"Ooh, a Red Sox fan?" James asked as if he either didn't hear, or care about what Anthony did for a living.

"I follow them. I'm not obsessed like some of the people up there, but I keep track of what's going on. I'm more of a hockey fan."

"I always wanted to see Fenway Park, but never had the chance," James noted.

"I've been there a handful of times," Anthony said. "It's everything they say. "Usually I've gone there with clients."

"You ever go with your dad?"

"Ah, I've never gone with my step-dad."

"I'm sorry, I don't mean to pry," James said.

"No problem. I never actually knew my biological father. My stepfather died some years back. He battled cancer off and on for five years. He was a good man – good to my mom. He was serious and hard working, not really the sensitive kind. But, he really was my dad."

Anthony continued. "Listen to me – you don't want to hear about this."

"It sounds like your mom did a great job."

"She absolutely did," Anthony said proudly. "She sacrificed a lot for us. I guess it's our time to take care of her now."

"Well, if your mom ever needs anything, there are a lot of people here to help." James tried to make Anthony feel at ease.

"Thanks very much. I appreciate that. Well, I better get going. It was nice meeting you."

James was sorry to see him leave. He had immediately felt a connection he had not felt in a long time.

CHAPTER 5

A few days had passed. Jennifer, Jacqui and Anthony were there every day, usually around lunch and dinner. That was normal. They wanted to make sure their mom eased into this major transition.

Rosemont encouraged family members to visit often the first couple weeks. However, they also counseled family members concerning the consequences of visiting too much as time went on. The new resident needed to be acclimated to their new surroundings and their "new family" without a lot of interference.

James overhead Anthony say that he would be going back to Boston the next morning. Mary advised him not to worry about her – she would be okay. Jennifer and Jacqui knew things would fall on their shoulders. They'd been taking care of Mary.

After dinner, Mary and her children took a walk to the pond. There were a few rocking chairs and a glider. It was a very quiet area and was always well maintained.

From afar, James could see the gazebo from his room.

James knew it would be very difficult for Anthony to leave. At dinner, he could tell Anthony seemed very uneasy and restless. He said all the rights things about coming back home as often as he could – but how often could he really do that?

Later that evening Anthony was walking through the halls in James' wing. He saw James in his room. He stopped and knocked on his door. James was already in bed, but was still awake.

"Sorry, Mr. Evans, I just wanted to say good-bye."

James started to sit up. "You have yourself a good trip. And try not to worry too much about things here."

"I'll do my best. I will try to make the trip back every few weeks or so – hopefully once a month.   I'll definitely be back on Thanksgiving.   I really hate to put this all on my sisters."

"Believe me, there's a lot of help here – your mom definitely won't be alone. There's always someone checking on you."

"Well, thank you. I appreciate that.   You take care of yourself, Mr. Evans."

James felt good about himself. In his mind, Anthony seemed a little better when he left. He didn't lie to Anthony – Mary would have all kinds of help. Of course, being alone, and feeling lonely, are two different things.

CHAPTER 6

Some days had passed. Nothing really earth shattering to report at Rosemont. It was late August. The warm days were starting to give way to some cooler nights. The hours of daylight were starting to get shorter.

To be honest, that fact really did not affect the residents. After supper, they were either in their rooms, in the main lobby, or strolling the halls. It wasn't like they were going to be playing bocce or going for bike rides late at night.

On this particular night James was sitting on the back deck of wing C. From there he could see someone sitting next to Rosemont's garden. He was finally able to determine it was Mary.

"Betsy, would I be able to go for a walk?"

Betsy Klein was one of the aides. An aide always had to be with a resident if they were sitting outside.

"Really?"

"Yes."

"Sorry. I just seem surprised. I don't remember the last time you wanted to go for a walk. At least not during my shifts."

"I'm thinking outside of the box, Betsy."

"Ha! Where did you hear that phrase?"

"Hey, honey, I watch Dr. Phil."

"Okay, Doc. Where do you want to go?"

"How about out front, around the corner?"

Betsy advised Rosie at the front desk that she was taking James outside.

"Well, I'll be damned," she said. "Mr. Evans is actually going for a walk. I think I'll have to write this down."

"Ha ha ha, "James replied, sarcastically.

"Betsy, you guys best be going before he changes his mind."

"We're out of here," Betsy said.

Betsy pushed James in his wheelchair. At the end of the front parking lot, there was a V-shaped pathway.

"Where would you like to go from here, Mr. Evans?"

"Ah, let's try right."

They went around towards the back of wing B.

"Looks like someone is already out here," Betsy noted.

"I wonder who it is," James said as if he didn't know.

"Oh, it's Mary Hubert. You want to go say hi, Mr. Evans?"

"Yeah, why not?"

Mary was with Hanna.

"Hey, look who's out here," Hanna said. "I don't remember the last time I've seen you on a walk, Mr. Evans."

"That seems to be the consensus," James said.

"Good evening, Mr. Evans."

"Hello, Mary. How are you doing tonight?"

"Oh, not too bad, I guess."

Betsy leaned over to Hannah. "Hey, did you just hear about the changes they're planning to make to the Bonus program?"

"Hah! Don't even get me started about that," Hannah said.

Betsy looked at Mary and James. "Why don't you guys talk? Hannah and I will be right back there, gossiping." Betsy had pointed to a bench that was about 15 feet behind them.

As Betsy and Hannah complained about some changes Rosemont was proposing, James found himself in an awkward position. He had wanted to come out and see her, but now that he was here, he found himself at a loss for words.

Mary took care of that.

"They have such a beautiful garden," Mary stated.

"Yeah, I didn't realize it was this big."

"They've pulled some of the tomatoes and cucumbers. It looks like that row over there was lettuce. I guess it's time for most of the garden to be picked, with September coming."

"What's that over there?" James asked, as he pointed to the right side of the garden.

"Looks like spinach, perhaps," Mary said. "Hey, look behind that – I actually think they are trying to grow some pumpkins."

"Yeah, I think you're right. I wonder how many they expect?"

"I don't know. It was always my experience that pumpkins weren't the easiest thing to grow in a small garden."

"You had planted before, Mary?"

"Oh, we always had a garden. When I was a kid, we had one. It was my father who actually did the planting. When I was married, we always had a big garden."

"I talked to your son before he left. He spoke highly of your husband."

"He was a good man. He worked really hard," she said. James did not let on that he knew that her husband was actually Anthony's step-father.

"Your whole family seems very nice. Your daughters sure seem like hard workers."

"Thank you. I don't know what I would do without them. This is all so new. It's really overwhelming at this point."

"It is. Over time you'll start getting used to things." James realized he was trying to reassure Mary, much as he did with Anthony.

CHAPTER 7

Mary became more acclimated to Rosemont as the weeks past.

She befriended Erma Jones. Erma had been at the facility for a short time. She was definitely not a lifer, but she knew her way around. She was quiet and didn't cause any problems. Her husband died about five years ago. He had been in deteriorating health, and Erma pretty much took care of him herself. Their children rarely visited. Mary felt so much empathy for Erma. Although she didn't say it to Erma, her children were spoiled. Erma seemed like such a gracious, compassionate person. She deserved better.

While the weather was still pretty decent in October, Mary and Erma took nightly strolls to the pond. They sat on the bench and watched the ducks paddle their way downstream. They talked about everything from their families, their youth, to their favorite color. They became extremely close. Jacqui and Jennifer were very grateful for Erma's friendship with their mom. They were sure it made Mary's transition to Rosemont much easier.

James pretty much knew Erma as another face in the crowd. But since Mary had arrived, and befriended Erma, James got to know her better.

With Halloween coming up, Rosemont was decked out in skeletons, pumpkins, witches and vampires. It was very decorative. You could always count on some of the staff to dress festively each day as well.

A few days before Halloween, family and friends were invited to visit for trick or treating. Families were encouraged to bring their children, grandchildren and nieces and nephews. It provided the kids a safe place to trick or treat, and it was an opportunity for the residents to interact with others outside the facility. It was an interesting juxtaposition – the residents enjoyed seeing the little kids, while most of the kids were initially scared of the residents. Most kids had not seen so many people in wheelchairs.

Rosemont held a "best dressed" contest for the residents. About half participated, so that was considered a huge success by the staff. Prior to the kids showing up, the results were announced. Erma finished second. With the help of some of the staff, she was dressed like a princess. They worked on her hair and put makeup on her. She looked really beautiful, and much younger.

Dorothy Masterson took first place. She was dressed as a witch – which most people thought matched her personality. Most thought Erma should have won. They rationalized that many of the residents were afraid not to vote to Dorothy.

James got involved – which was a surprise to many. They could tell Erma and Mary - especially Mary, were having a positive impact on him. One of the cooks brought in his son's football equipment. James dressed as a football player. He had the shoulder pads, jersey and helmet. It was a bitch to get the jersey over his shoulder pads, so they told him he had to wear it at least a couple hours!

Mary put on her Halloween sweatshirt. That was good enough for her.

The residents would sit outside their rooms as the kids walked through the halls. The residents were provided with candy to hand out. James decided to go to where Mary and Erma were sitting. Some of the kids would stare at James. They had never seen an old man in a football uniform. He did get some smiles, though. One little boy took an interest.

"Who do you play for?" the boy asked.

James laughed heartily. "Oh, I haven't played in years. But thanks for asking."

"Who's your favorite team?" the boy asked.

"Oh, I'm an old Steelers fan."

The boy looked up at his mom. "Mom, did you hear that? He's a Steelers' fan too."

"I heard," his mom said.

"What is your name?" James asked the boy.

"Timmy." He was dressed as a fireman.

"Well, it's nice to meet you, Timmy. I like your costume. That's a very noble profession."

"We got to ride on a fire truck at school."

"You did?"

"Yep. A fireman gave me this hat."

"He wears it everywhere," his mom said. "It was just natural that he would be a fireman for Halloween."

"We get to trick or treat at school tomorrow," Timmy said to Mary.

"Really? That sounds like fun."

"You didn't dress up," he said to Mary.

"I have on my Halloween sweatshirt. I'm a pumpkin."

"Oh." It didn't seem like a costume to Timmy.

James put extra candy in Timmy's bag. "Maybe you'll play football when you get bigger."

"I want to play for the Steelers."

"Good for you."

"Did you used to play for the Steelers?"

"No, no. I didn't get that far. I played for West Cannon."

"West Cannon?" Mary asked quickly.

"Yeah. You've heard of them?"

"They were always good in football. I used to go to a lot of their games when I was young."

"Oh yeah? Who knows – maybe you saw me play," James said with a laugh.

"Well, we better keep moving, Timmy," his mom said. "I think we're holding up the line."

"It was very nice meeting you," Mary said.

"Thanks for talking to us," James said.

"What a pleasant little boy," Erma added.

As they left, Mary turned to James. "So you played for West Cannon?"

"Yes. It was the best time in my life. Everything went downhill after that."

CHAPTER 8

THANKSGIVING DAY

They were right. The house was very big. It was too much house for one person, even someone in good health. This was the house where Mary and her late husband, Ted, raised their family. As the kids helped James and Erma into the front door, James could sense an emptiness right away. There were still some furniture and appliances, but the house felt "cold" in every sense of the word.

But, this wasn't about James. All eyes were on Mary. How would she handle seeing her home for the first time in several weeks?

So far, so good. As she entered, the first thing she did was ask that the furnace be turned up. From the outside, she didn't seem too emotional. She asked for some water, and that the coffee pot be turned on. It was as if she had never left.

Jennifer and Jacqui went right to work, preparing the meal. They made sure it was the typical Thanksgiving dinner – turkey, stuffing, mashed potatoes, rolls, cranberry, and corn.

Jacqui looked at James and Erma. "I understand it's been a long time since you've had a Thanksgiving dinner?"

"Yes, this is just overwhelming," Erma said.

James didn't want to hurt anyone's feelings, and was afraid to tell her that Rosemont seemed to serve turkey, stuffing and potatoes every few weeks. *But, there was nothing like a Thanksgiving dinner at someone's home, surrounded by younger people,* James thought to himself. He couldn't remember the last time he had been in an actual home, let alone celebrating a holiday.

Make no mistake – this was Mary's day. But, undoubtedly James may have felt more of a culture shock. After all, it wasn't that long ago that Mary was living in this house.

After dinner, James and Anthony sat in the den and watched a football game. Anthony kept his laptop and Blackberry close to him. It was evident that work was important to him, even on a holiday. James also talked to Erma, and got to know her a little better. He was happy that Mary had found a friend in Erma.

Jennifer popped into the den. "Who wants dessert? We've got pumpkin pie, cherry pie, and chocolate pie."

Chocolate seemed to be the overwhelming favorite.

"Jennifer, may I use the bathroom?" James asked.

"Certainly, Mr. Evans. Do you need some help?"

"Just to the bathroom. I just wanted to wash my hands."

Jacqui spoke up. "I can help you, Mr. Evans. You can use the bathroom next to Mom's room. There's a lot more room than the other bathroom."

"Not to mention the other one is on the second floor," added Jennifer.

"Oooh yeah, that would be difficult," noted James. "It would take me quite a while to get up the stairs."

James noticed the décor of the old-fashioned bathroom. The mirrored door on the medicine cabinet opened by sliding it back and forth. The walls were filled with little ceramic tiles half way up.

There was a border near the top of the walls – tan with light blue flowers.

He also noticed some old jewelry at one end of the vanity. The jewelry had been piled up, as if someone just threw it there without going through it.

And that's when he saw it.

The shock hit him like a train. He started having trouble breathing normally. Jacqui could hear him sort of gagging.

"Are you alright, Mr. Evans?"

He barely heard her. So many things were running through his mind. *It couldn't be, it couldn't be,* he kept telling himself.

By this time Jacqui had called for Anthony.

"Mr. Evans – you okay? I'm coming in," Anthony said in a booming voice.

Anthony entered, and saw Mr. Evans hunched over the sink. "Let me help you, Mr. Evans."

"I gotta go….I gotta go," was all James kept trying to say.

"To the bathroom?" Anthony asked. "You have to go to the bathroom?"

"No, no," James said anxiously. "I…I can't stay. I have to leave. I have to leave now."

By then, Jennifer had come over to see what the noise was about.

"Mr. Evans, do you want to sit down?" Jacqui asked. "We can sit you in the recliner in Mom's room."

"No. I'm sorry, but I have to go now."

"Do you want to eat your pie first?" Jennifer asked.

"No," James said, somewhat forcefully. "I really need to get back."

Anthony drove James back to Rosemont. He kept looking over at James, but James did not say a word. Anthony met with John Geiner at the nurses' station. He was the head nurse who had night duty.

"Mr. Evans, back so soon?" John asked. "We weren't expecting you until later."

James just looked up at John, and mumbled something. A couple of aides took over and helped James back to his room.

Anthony waited until James was out of hearing distance. "I don't know what happened," he said to John. "We thought he was doing pretty well. And, then all of a sudden, he panicked, and wanted to come back."

"Well, I'm no psychologist," John noted. "But it would not be the first time I have heard of such a thing. I think it may have hit him where he was, and he could have had a panic attack. This is his comfort zone here. This is the only place he's really known for so long now."

John was a very well respected nurse at Rosemont. But time and events would prove that he should probably stay out of the psychology field. Neither he nor Anthony could have guessed what made James panic. Soon they would find out.

CHAPTER 9

James didn't sleep much that night. He tried to put it out of his mind, but it was not possible. What were the chances of this happening?

He rang the "cow bell," as it was called -- the button that residents could push when they needed assistance.

Hannah Russell responded "You rang, Mr. Evans? Are you ready to go to breakfast?"

"Hannah, I'm not hungry. Can you take me to the chapel?"

"The chapel?" She seemed very surprised. "I don't think I have ever seen you go down there."

She was right. It was at least five years since James had visited the chapel. It was located downstairs. A small percentage of the residents visited the chapel on a somewhat regular basis, but most residents did not. Parishioners from some of the local churches visited Rosemont to deliver communion and pray with the residents.

"Do you want the kitchen to bring a tray to your room a little later, then?"

"That would be fine," James noted.

Hannah alerted the kitchen, and then took James to the chapel. She waited outside. James was seated in the front pew.

"Hello."

James was startled.

"I'm sorry. I didn't mean to scare you."

"Oh, I didn't know anyone was here," James said. "I can leave."

"No, I wouldn't think of it. Please, stay as long as you want. 'I'm Pastor Jonah, by the way."

"Nice to meet you, Pastor. I'm James Evans."

"I'll be out of your way, Mr. Evans, and you can have some quiet."

The chapel was small, maybe 20 pews or so. There was a small altar, with candles on both sides. A large cross hung on the back wall.

It was suddenly very quiet. James stared at the cross. He began to cry, somewhat uncontrollably. He realized it had been a long time since he had cried this hard.

"Forgive me Lord, for not coming here more often. I know I should pray more. I don't know what to do. I need a sign."

He really didn't think he would receive a sign, but he felt desperate. What he saw at Mary's house – he knew he needed help – divine help. James had felt that God abandoned him a long time ago. He was stuck in this nursing home, and he had been alone for so long. *Maybe God owes me one*, he thought.

He sat back in the pew. He had calmed down. He looked at the cross and remembered what the priests and nuns had said when he was a kid. Jesus died for our sins. Everyone would have their share of suffering on earth. James was no exception. But why were things so unfair? Why did he suffer more than most, he asked himself. Why was God putting this on his shoulders? What did He want James to do?

CHAPTER 10

The Sunday after Thanksgiving, James again requested a visit to the chapel. He sat in the same, front row pew. Suddenly a man appeared.

"Well, hello, Mr. Evans."

"Oh, Pastor, I didn't see you. I just came in to say a prayer."

"Take all the time you want. You are always welcome."

"Thank you. I like it here. I wish I would have been coming more often."

"It's never too late."

James smiled. He figured a pastor would say something like that.

"Pastor, can I ask you something?"

"Absolutely. What's on your mind, son?"

Son? James had to laugh to himself. How long had it been since he was called that?

The pastor sat in the front row, across from James.

"Do you really believe that God forgives all sins?"

"I do. But I also believe a person has to be honest with himself. Is he remorseful for his sins? Has he tried to make amends?"

"In other words, God doesn't have a magic wand."

The pastor let out a laugh. "That's a good way of putting it. I believe God forgives all sins, but we also have to do our part."

"But how do we make amends for things we may have done years ago? We can't go back."

"That's a great question. You're right. If only we could go back in time – to right our wrongs."

"Then, there's really nothing we can do," James deduced.

"Not necessarily. God still gives us a special gift."

"What's that?"

"Today. He gives us today. Can a person still do something today that will make a difference? Is there anything in particular you would like to talk about, Mr. Evans? I'm a great listener."

James had to smile. He felt at ease with the pastor, but wasn't ready to "spill his guts."

"You are a great listener. I'm sorry – I sound like some kid who's confused about life."

"Don't be sorry. None of us are too old to learn. And I believe there is no age limit on wisdom. I'll be right back," the pastor said. He went into the back room, to the side of the altar. He came back with a small book.

"Here's something that I think you might find interesting."

"What is it?" James asked.

"Well, I don't want to give too many details. I'd like you to read it. Basically it's about a man who is learning to deal with choices he made long ago."

James scanned the cover, looking for the author.

"Oh, you won't find the author's name. It's anonymous. But he's an excellent writer."

"Okay. Thank you. I appreciate you taking the time to talk."

"Any time, Mr. Evans."

As the Pastor left, a thought struck James. *The author is "anonymous", yet the pastor said "he" is an excellent writer......*

CHAPTER 11

For the first time that the staff could recall, there seemed to be legitimate concern about James. He had his moments, like all residents. But he was always on a pretty even keel, and the staff generally knew what to expect from him.

He hadn't been eating much. He seemed less talkative with the other residents, and now he was requesting visits to the chapel. Some of the staff thought that perhaps his kidneys were starting to worsen, and he was having some type of "come to Jesus" moment.

On a Friday night, as the snow was starting to fly, Mary came by James' room.

"Mind if I visit?" she asked.

James was startled. He started to get butterflies in his stomach – the same kind youngsters get when they experience their first love. He really hadn't talked to Mary much since the Thanksgiving Day debacle – a fact that wasn't missed on Mary.

"I haven't talked to you in a while, James. They said you haven't been feeling well. I just wanted to see how you were doing."

"Yeah, I guess I've been under the weather lately. I apologize for Thanksgiving."

"No need to. We were glad you were able to come over." She took a seat next to the television.

"What's on tonight?" she asked.

"I'm just watching a college football game."

"I enjoy college football. It's exciting."

James felt uncomfortable. He wasn't sure if this was the right time. His instincts said "no."

"I don't know what I'd do without sports on TV," James said, trying to make some small talk.

"Are you originally from around here, James?" she asked.

"No. How about you?" James asked, not answering the obvious question as to where he was from, and lying at the same time.

"I'm from this area. When I was a little girl, I went to Crestfield High."

James already knew that. But he decided now was not the time to tell her that.

"Do you have any brothers or sisters?" Mary asked.

"I have one sister."

"How about you?"

"I was an only child. I guess I was spoiled. When I was young I knew I wanted more than one child."

"Do you have any children, James?"

"I had a baby daughter. She died of SIDS at five months."

"Oh, my goodness, I am so sorry to hear that. That must have been absolutely difficult to deal with."

"It was. It was also the beginning of the end of my marriage. We were so excited to have a child......and then to have it taken away just like that. My wife and I never were the same after that."

Mary had tears in her eyes.

James paused. "I remember people thinking I should just get over it – because we only had her for a short time. As if she was "on loan". I never got over it."

This was the first time James had opened up like that in quite some time. He was realizing that since Mary arrived, nothing was going to be the same for him again. The comfort zone he had long been accustomed to was long gone.

CHAPTER 12
December 24 -- Christmas Eve

The day started like any other – up, cleaned up and dressed, in time for breakfast at 8:00. However, there was a certain buzz in the air. Many of the aides and cafeteria staff wore Christmas sweaters or shirts and Santa hats. There was no question they would have preferred being home on Christmas Eve, but they figured working first shift on this day was a hell of a lot better than second shift.

The more experienced staff knew that some of the residents had little or no family. Regardless of their age, and what they may say, nobody really wanted to be all alone on Christmas.

James was asked by Mary's family if he wanted to join them, and a couple of the other residents at Jacqui's house. If nothing else it was an opportunity to get out of the nursing home for a few hours. But James told them he had been invited by William Hersh's family for a Christmas Eve dinner.

James lied. There had been no such invitation. He knew he would not be comfortable if he had gone with Mary's family. It would be impossible. Plus he couldn't keep it to himself any longer – he needed to talk to Mary.

CHAPTER 13

Santa Claus arrived after lunch. The staff knew that most of the residents would not be leaving with family members until later in the day. Perfect time now for Santa to entertain the residents.

He had goodies – hand lotion, shampoos, new bingo chips and lottery tickets. James could not comprehend the lottery tickets. Even if one of them won, the winner would be either too old or too sick to enjoy it. But it was Christmas and strange gifts were part of the holiday mystique. At Rosemont, it was no different.

Almost two-thirds of the residents had family members who visited this day. The rest had no visitors.

A choir from the local Assembly Church provided beautiful Christmas music. Santa joined in. James sat there and wondered how many choirs this had been – he figured this was the fifth or sixth choir in December. The residents' monthly fees hard at work, James thought.

Everyone knows Christmas is magical for children. For James, it was a myth. He could not remember the last time he truly enjoyed Christmas. Even when he was married, his wife made it seem more like a chore. Certainly, after losing their baby daughter, there would be no more holiday celebrations.

But it wasn't always that way. Growing up, James loved Christmas. Actually, it was his favorite time of year. His father was a foreman at a large manufacturing plant. He worked long hours. As a kid, James wondered if his father even knew what holiday it was. He ended up dying young.

His mother was different. Every December 1, she made it a point to start bringing up the Christmas boxes from the cellar. She enjoyed everything about the holiday – and not just the shopping, baking and wrapping. She was able to find time to reflect on the spiritual part of the season. She had a devout faith. She felt God would take care of everything.

It was her passion that influenced James. Her energy was contagious. As a kid, he enjoyed the anticipation of Christmas. He would sit in the living room late at night with just the Christmas lights on. His parents and sister would already be in bed. He would hum carols. He would envision what Christmas would be when he got older. A big house, heavily decorated. Lots of Christmas cookies. Certainly, a large family opening presents early Christmas morning. He would let his mind enter a realm of unlimited possibilities.

And now here he was, wondering how it all went wrong.

CHAPTER 14

Many of the residents had left by supper time. Some of them were going to Christmas services with their families. For the residents that remained, it was eerily quiet. The aides tried their best to keep up the spirits of those remaining. But, they were experienced enough to know that you could not manufacture holiday spirit. They knew they were not getting visitors for Christmas. The best they could do is simply be there for the remaining residents.

James sat in his recliner. He shut the lights off and asked that his door be closed most of the way. He started watching 'It's A Wonderful Life." He kept switching between that and "Scrooge." It seemed like he had watched them just about every Christmas Eve since he had been at Rosemont. It was his holiday "tradition."

He picked up the book the Pastor gave him. He turned off the TV, and turned on his night light. After a couple hours, he had finished the book. The Pastor was right – it was an excellent read. He realized the main character in the book faced many of the same challenges as James.

It was almost 11:00. James wondered if Mary had come back. James buzzed the nurses' station. Gloria Hawthorne was working the night shift. She had only been at Rosemont for a little over a year.

"What can I do for you, Mr. Evans?"

"I was wondering if you could help me with something."

"Sure, you name it."

James pulled out a necklace from his drawer.

"Wow, that's pretty," Gloria noted.

"Would it be possible to wrap it for me?"

"Oooh, who's the lucky lady?"

James did not have the energy to talk about it. "If you could please do that, I would really appreciate it."

"No problem. I'll take care of it right now. Merry Christmas, Mr. Evans."

"Thank you."

CHAPTER 15

DECEMBER 25 – CHRISTMAS

On Christmas Day, Rosemont served a holiday brunch at 10:00. Families were invited. As quiet as it was just 15 hours ago, it was just as loud now. For as low key as last night's staff seemed, this first shift staff was very upbeat. And, their job was to try to keep the residents upbeat, as well.

Anthony and his wife, Lori, and their daughter, Kristy, came into town for a few days. They knew his mom needed continued support, especially with this being her first official Christmas in a nursing home.

"Merry Christmas, Mr. Evans."

"Merry Christmas, Anthony. When did you get in?"

"Late yesterday afternoon. We'll probably stay 3 or 4 days."

"Are your sisters here?"

"No. I'll be taking Mom to my aunt's house. We're all going to meet there later. What about you?"

"Oh…I have a nephew who's going to be picking me up later. I'm going to his house – big feast, lots of presents." Again, James lied.

"Well, you enjoy yourself, then," Anthony said.

"Thank you. Tell your mom I said to have a Merry Christmas."

The brunch was actually very good. Rosemont went all out – eggs, ham, potatoes, rolls, carved beef, and various salads. *It looks like a lot of leftovers for the residents this week*, James thought to himself.

James spent the afternoon as if it were any other day. And it would be, except for all the commercials reminding him it's Christmas.

He did notice a light snow around 4:00. The sky was gray, somewhat gloomy. The wind was starting to pick up a little. The weatherman said there was a possibility of a few inches of snow by late tonight. James thought back to those days when a snowfall on Christmas day was magical. It seemed to deliver a spirit within people that few things could match. As a kid he wished that feeling would never go away. As an adult, he couldn't wait until it was over.

James decided tonight would be the night. When Mary came back, he would have to talk to her. Maybe the spirit of Christmas would make things go easier, he reasoned. But then, maybe it wouldn't...

CHAPTER 16

When Mary came back to Rosemont, James waited until her family had left. He came by her room, and asked her how her day went.

"Hello – oh, didn't mean to startle you. Just wondering how your Christmas day was."

"Oh, I had a nice time. It was a really nice day," Mary said.

"Good. I'm glad to hear that."

"And how about you – Anthony told me you were spending the day at your nephew's."

James didn't say anything. He looked at Mary and then looked down.

"Mary, I don't know if now is the right time. I don't know if there is any good time. But, I need to talk to you."

Mary seemed justifiably confused. "You can come in. You know I think I'm over tired – it was a tiring day, but I don't feel like sleeping. Might be all the coffee I drank," Mary said, as she laughed.

"Mary, I didn't go to my nephew's today. I have a nephew but he doesn't live here. I haven't seen him in years. Truth be told – I didn't leave Rosemont yesterday night, either."

"I don't understand," Mary said. "Oh, I feel awful. You were by yourself for Christmas? You were more than welcome to come with us."

"I know…and I appreciate that."

Mary noticed that James now seemed nervous, and uncomfortable.

"I have something to tell you. Actually, I have something to show you."

James continued. "I have struggled with this. I wasn't sure what to do. I'm still not convinced this is the right thing to do."

James pulled something from his pajama pocket. As he gave it to Mary, he simply said, "I'm sorry, Mary."

"What is it?" Mary asked.

"Open it, please."

Mary unwrapped it. "My, what a pretty box."

As she opened the box, James could feel his heart beating faster. When Mary opened it, she just stared at it. She then put her right hand to her mouth. After she caught her breath, she looked at James.

"My God....no. This can't be."

She looked at the box, and then back at James. "Jimmy?"

"It's me, Mary. It's Jimmy."

She started to cry. It was the cry of someone who has been emotionally destroyed. She continued to look at James. It was as if she was looking through James.

Inside the box was a necklace with a gold half a heart. On it was inscribed, "My Mary."

"Mary, I've kept that all these years – and I know you kept yours."

"How did you know?"

"On Thanksgiving, when I was at your house, I had gone into the bathroom. There was a bunch of jewelry piled up. I wasn't going through your jewelry – believe me. I just saw the other half of the heart."

"My Jimmy?"

"That's right. It was inscribed "My Jimmy." The 'I' was dotted with a small heart."

"That's why you left in such a hurry, wasn't it?"

"Yes. I didn't know what to do."

"You've known since Thanksgiving, and you haven't said anything?" Mary asked, somewhat forcefully.

"Believe me, I've been thinking about this day and night. I wasn't sure if I should say anything after all this time."

"So, why now? Why are you showing me this now?"

James was starting to stutter his words. "Deep down, I just felt like it was the right thing to do. I guess I just felt like you had a right to know."

Mary sat back as she rubbed her hands through her hair. She was not crying as hard. Now, she seemed more upset.

"So, what now? What were you expecting me to say now?"

"I'm not sure. I really don't know what I thought would happen. My heart told me it was the right thing to tell you."

"Your heart? Your heart? Where was your heart when you left me all alone?"

Mary looked out her window, and thought about that very special time so many years ago...

CHAPTER 17

..1960

Harley's Drive-In

"Here they come," yelled Rhonda, as she flipped back the shade and sat back down. Rhonda Sue Perkins (she despised the "Sue" part), Barbara Taft, Joanie Sestak and Mary Hubert – members of the "Queen Of Hearts " club. At least that is what the back of their jackets said. Seems like just about everyone was part of a club. If you weren't, what was wrong with you?

There was no better place to show off your jackets than at Harley's. Ben Harley was to the restaurant business what Dick Clark was to Bandstand. Ben never grew up, and although he was about to turn 45, he acted every bit like the young kids that patronized his drive-in. He was single – there was no time for a wife. The kids at Harley's were his family.

The burgers at Harley's were nothing to write home about, but this was the place to go after school.

The girls of the "Queen Of Hearts" were giddy. The coolest senior at West Cannon High was walking in. Stevie Johns was cool. Just ask him. He was West Cannon's "Fonzie." Tight jeans, tee shirt, and greased back long hair. He was every girl's fantasy, and every mother's worst nightmare. He didn't do very well in school. It was not that he was stupid. He definitely had the street smarts. He just didn't apply himself, and school was not a priority in his life. He was good at two things – picking up girls, and fixing cars.

With him were Lenny Parks, Jerry Sullivan, and James "Jim" Evans.

"Ladies, good to see you," Stevie said, as the boys crowded in the booth next to the girls.

Rhonda Sue had the biggest crush on Stevie. She was always writing love letters to him – which she would never send. She felt that if she could keep the fantasy alive, they would eventually be together.

The boys didn't have jackets. They didn't belong to a club. They didn't have to. When you hung out with Stevie Johns, it was already understood that you were cool.

Jim knew Rhonda and Barbara from West Cannon. He had seen Joanie and Mary around, but had never formally met them. As the girls and boys talked over the booth, Mary found herself staring at Jim. Jim was athletic looking. He was of medium height, but had a wide neck and big chest. He had brown, wavy hair, with just a little bit of curl to it. Every once in a while she caught him glancing her way.

Although Stevie did not feel exactly the same way about Rhonda Sue as she felt about him, he did like dancing with her. He put some money in the jukebox, and they, along with Barbara, Joanie, Lenny and Jerry, started dancing.

"Come on, you guys, don't be a couple of stiffs," Rhonda Sue said to Mary and Jim.

"No, thanks," Mary and Jim said in unison. They looked at each other and laughed. Mary then motioned for Jim to come over to her booth.

"Hi, I'm Mary Hubert."

Jim shook her hand. "Jim...Jim Evans – nice to meet you. I think I've seen you around."

"Yeah, I've started coming here more often, now that I'm a senior," Mary noted.

"What school do you go to?" James asked.

"Crestfield."

"Ah, home of the Fightin' Crusaders."

"Yep, that's the one," she said, with a chuckle.

"I go to West Cannon."

"I know," Mary said.

"How did you know?"

"I've seen your picture in the newspaper, for football. Plus I have some friends at West Cannon. I end up going to a lot of the football games."

"A traitor at heart," James noted.

"No, my heart is still with Crestfield. But, we're so bad at football, it's tough to watch our games."

"Yeah, I wasn't going to bring that up," James said. "But, we pretty much have had our way with you guys the last few years."

"Who hasn't?" Mary reminded him.

They laughed again.

They were both becoming very comfortable talking to each other. Most of the boys Mary knew were stuck up, perverted, or both. She had a sense that Jim was different.

After a few moments, Jim got the courage to ask Mary to dance.

"Would you like to join your friends on the dance floor?" he asked.

"Well, I'm not much of a dancer. I get embarrassed easily. But, if a slow song comes on, I would dance."

That surprised Jim. He smiled at her. Luckily, Jerry took a break to drink his soda, when he overheard their conversation. He immediately went over to the jukebox, and pressed a couple slow songs. Good ol' Jerry.

"Oh, as fate would have it, here's your slow song," Jim said to Mary. "Would you care to dance?"

"Sure!" They danced to Sam Cook's 'It's A Wonderful World." It sure felt wonderful at that moment.

CHAPTER 18

That night at Harley's led to Mary and Jim's first date. Their first date would include dinner at Damon's Italian Restaurant, and then a movie at the Castle Movie Theater.

James arrived at Mary's house with his '57 Ford. He saved up for the car, having worked at Bennie's Market the past couple years.

Mary looked very pretty. She wore her hair down, and James noticed she had put on a little makeup. James met her parents – Bill and Anne Marie. They were typical middle class America. Bill had served in the Army. He now worked as a salesman for a large manufacturing company. Anne Marie stayed at home.

"Daddy, this is Jim."

'Hello, nice to meet you sir," Jim said, nervously.

"Jim? Hello." Bill shook Jim's hand.

Anne Marie came in from the kitchen. She had on her apron, which apparently wasn't unusual. She was in the middle of baking a pie. Jim could see right away where Mary got her natural beauty.

They sat and talked for about 10 minutes. Bill didn't say much. Jim could tell Mary's dad was trying to size up Jim. Anne Marie was very down to earth, and did most of the talking.

Jim had told them his father worked in a tool and die plant, but that he had passed on. When he mentioned it, he could see the angst on Mary's face. He sensed that they were a very close family, and Mary would be devastated if anything like that happened in her family.

After the small talk, Jim and Mary headed for Damon's. For a Friday night, it wasn't crowded. Damon's was not a cheap date, but Jim wanted to make sure he impressed Mary – this being their first date and all. Damon's had a fireplace in the main dining room. The décor included candles, with flowers around them, at each table, and fancy table cloths.

"This is really something, Jim. We didn't need to go to such a fancy restaurant."

She noticed! Jim perked up. Not many 17-year-olds could take their dates to a restaurant like this – not unless it was the Prom.

Jim tried ordering from the wine list, but was quickly shot down because of his youthful looks. *At least I gave it a try*, he thought.

Mary leaned over the table. "It must be tough not having a father around."

This wasn't the way he expected the conversation to start.

"Yeah, but it's not as bad as a couple years ago. At first, my mom was really messed up. She was always sad or angry. But, we've now gotten used to it being just me, my mom, and my sister."

"Are you guys close?"

This was more than young Jim expected to talk about. Initially, he was nervous that they would just sit and stare at each other, looking for conversation. That was no longer a concern.

"Well, my sister's older. So, we really don't have that much in common. I just try to get along with my mom – try to do what she asks. I have a lot of freedom. She usually doesn't give me a lot of grief when I want to go out."

Jim continued. "You close to your family? It seems like you are."

"Very much," Mary said.

"Do you have any sisters or brothers?" Jim asked.

"No, it's just me. My parents didn't have me until later. Sometimes it gets lonely. I wish I had a brother or sister to talk to, to share things with. But, I am close to my parents.

The waitress brought them their salads.

"So what's it like hanging out with the coolest kid?"

"Stevie? He's a good guy."

"How much of that is an act?" Mary was very perceptive.

"You can't tell him I said this, but he acts differently when everyone is around. When it's just me and him hanging out, he doesn't act like that."

"That's what I figured," Mary said.

"He just has a reputation that he has to uphold."

"My friend, Rhonda Sue, has a major crush on him."

"I could tell," James said. "Don't tell her this, but I don't think he feels the same way about her."

"Oh, I won't say anything. I wouldn't want to destroy her fantasies."

They both laughed.

"So, do you like Crestfield?" Jim asked.

"It's okay. We aren't as big as you guys."

"Yeah, WC is pretty big."

"It seems like you guys are always good in sports."

"Some sports, anyways. Like football."

"Yeah, yeah, we all know about West Cannon football…."

Jim laughed. "Best in the state."

"You're really good. I've seen you play."

"Thanks. I'm hoping it will help get me into college. I'll need a scholarship."

"Have you heard from any schools?"

"Yeah, I got letters from Ohio University and Buffalo. I also got an inquiry from Penn State."

"Wow, that's great."

"What about you, Mary?"

"What do you mean?"

"After high school, what do you want to do?"

Mary looked puzzled. "I'll probably just try to find a job somewhere."

"You don't want to go to college?" James asked.

"My family's old fashioned. My mom stays at home. I know I'll have to find a job before I get married. But after that I will probably be a homemaker."

"It doesn't have to be like that," James said in a hopeful manner.

Mary didn't seem like she had more to say, and turned the conversation to Jim. "So what do you want to study in college?" she asked.

"Engineering or architecture – something in that field. I'd like to build things. Who knows – someday you might be driving over a bridge that I designed."

Mary didn't doubt him. Although he was just 17, James had a real confidence about him.

The waitress brought out their meals. They ate near the fireplace, and enjoyed each other's company.

At the movie theater, things weren't so comfortable. Jim knew it would be up to him to make a move. He very much wanted to hold her hand or put his arm around her. But this was their first date...and he didn't want it to be their last. So, he held back, spending the time wondering what Mary was thinking, and wondering if she wanted him to make a move.

The movie was short, so he had Mary home sooner than expected. James thought that would be a sign of respect to her parents. Jim walked Mary to her front door.

"Well, I had a good time, Jim. Dinner was great."

"Thanks. Me too," James said, somewhat nervously. "I had fun."

Mary got closer to James, and looked directly into his eyes. He could sense that she wanted him to kiss her. James reached for her hands, and they clenched. He stepped closer and kissed her. It wasn't a long kiss...but it was their first kiss.

CHAPTER 19

James and Mary started seeing each other more regularly. Most of the time they hung out at Harley's. Sometimes they would go to the theater. As it started to get a little warmer in April, they would drive to Lake Erie's Peninsula. It was way too early to swim, but Mary would pack a basket and they would enjoy lunch. They would spread a large blanket on the sand, and just talk.

It was there on a Friday night that James asked Mary if she would like to go to the Junior/Senior prom at West Cannon.

The night of the dance was something neither would forget. When James arrived at Mary's house, he was speechless. Mary was the most beautiful girl he had ever seen. She wore her hair up. She wore a pearl necklace – no doubt, something her mom had given her. She had on high heels. She was stunning.

"Why, hello there, Jim. Please come in," her mom said.

"Thanks."

"You look very handsome. I like your vest."

"Thank you, ma'am."

Mary and her mom went upstairs. "We'll be right down. Make yourself at home."

Her father walked in and shook James' hand.

"Where are you going for dinner?" he asked.

James was certain he already knew where they were going, but figured her father was just as uncomfortable, and was trying to make conversation.

"We're going to meet some friends at the Stone Village."

"That's a nice restaurant."

James nodded in agreement.

In the time that they had been dating, James figured he had only talked to Mary's father three or four times. He wasn't sure if her father cared for him, or if he just couldn't get used to the fact that his daughter was dating.

Mary came downstairs. James pinned the corsage on her.

Dinner was a lot of fun. At least on this night, the four members of the "Queen Of Hearts" who were at Harley's the night Mary and James met would be escorted by James's friends. Barbara Taft would be escorted by Jerry Sullivan. Joannie Sestak was Lenny Parks' date. And, unbelievably Rhonda Sue Perkins would be attending the dance with Stevie Johns. It's not that Stevie didn't have his pick of girls. He wanted to go with his friends, and Rhonda Sue had kept hounding him. She actually asked him to the dance. Rhonda Sue could care less about his reasons for saying "yes." She just knew that for at least one night, Stevie Johns was hers.

They laughed until their stomachs were hurting. James and Mary kept squeezing their hands underneath the table. They were happy to share the night with their friends. But they also knew that there was something special developing between them that the others did not have.

"The Jersey Boys" was a popular band at that time. They were a local band. None of the four band members were from New Jersey – and none had actually visited the state. But, they thought the name sounded cool. The band played a number of slow songs, and that suited James and Mary just fine.

"Jesus, Evans, we can't separate you guys tonight." Stevie said loudly. "We can find a minister and get you guys hitched."

"Oh my God – I would love to see to see your father's face if that happened," Rhonda Sue said to Mary.

James and Mary looked at each other. James thought for a moment what it would be like asking him for his daughter's hand in marriage.

"I would love to be there to see that," Stevie mused.

"Enough, you guys," James shot back.

One thing was apparent – James and Mary had become quite an item.

James wanted to make sure this was night was extra special. He realized how many times Mary had called him "her Jimmy." Although he never really said anything about it, he thought it was a cute nickname.

After the dance, James and Mary drove to the Lighthouse, located near the entrance to the east bay. It was well lit, and there was a boardwalk that led up to the area. It was very romantic, especially on an early summer's evening.

There was a light breeze, and the waves were hitting against the pier. Mary had put on her white sweater. She stood with her arms folded, looking across Lake Erie, towards Canada. James took out something from his suit pocket.

"This is for you."

"What's this?" Mary asked.

"Open it."

Mary's initial reaction is all James needed to see. "Oh, it's beautiful."

"I hope you like it."

"I love it. I love it."

James had given her a gold half-a-heart engraved with the words, "My Jimmy."

"You even dotted the "I" with a small heart," Mary said.

"Yeah, I noticed that when you spell my name you do it that way."

"Where's the other part?" she asked.

James reached into his shirt pocket and pulled out a necklace. It was the other half of the heart, engraved with the words, "My Mary."

Mary understood this was a huge step. It meant that James had committed himself only to her. She didn't need jewelry to confirm that, but this left no doubt. They kissed and James held her tight as the wind began to pick up.

CHAPTER 20

For James and Mary, the summer of 1960 was a fantasy.

When they were not spending time at the beaches, they could be found at the Olympia Pool. The Olympia was right outside of the city limits. It was a very large pool, with varying degrees of depth. This allowed all ages to enjoy it. However, for the most part, it was a popular hang-out for teenagers. There was a large food and snack area. In another area, a large stereo with speakers played continuously so that the kids could dance.

The big bash was coming up – July 4th at the Lagoon cabins. You had to take canoes and paddle boats to get to the cabins, from the beaches. For James and many of his friends this would be a new experience. Many of the kids that would be there were incoming high school seniors.

Mary didn't want to, but she had to lie to her parents. She could not remember when she had done so in the past. There was no way her dad was going to allow her to spend July 4th night at the cabins. He trusted his daughter. But, he knew there would be alcohol. And, he really wasn't sure he trusted James. Mary told her parents that she and James were going to her friend, Mary Abbott's, house. She hated the idea of lying, and it was certainly not in her character. But, this was the kind of night she dreamed about. She was going to make sure she spent it with James.

"Hey, Evans, you made it!" shouted Chester Stewart. James' canoe was making its way closer to the shore. Chester was standing near the shore line, with a beer in his hand. *This should be a very interesting night,* James thought to himself.

"Damn right we made it," James shouted back.

"Mary, you look lovely as usual," Chester noted.

"You are so full of shit, Stewart," James said as he helped them pull the canoe to shore. "Keep your eyes on your own girl," James said, with a laugh.

Chester was West Cannon's star running back. His future was wide open, and he was already getting offers from several colleges. He had his choice, but he liked partying more than he liked running the football.

Chester gave James a bear hug. "I'm glad you guys could make it. Let the party begin," Chester said as he raised his beer. He was drinking the good stuff – Koehler's in a bottle. That was way before light beer was even a thought.

As nighttime fast approached, many people began to arrive. Friends of friends of friends. The word got around. They had built a large bonfire. Some of the guys raced the paddle boats to show off for the girls. They weren't very good, and were even worse after a few drinks.

There were plenty of firecrackers and sparklers, but everyone looked forward to the fireworks display. The city put on their annual fireworks show over the main dock area.

As it got dark, a chill filled the air. The weatherman said the weather would start changing that week. It was going to be cooler with quite a bit of rain. The heat wave was finally ending.

As the fireworks started, everyone took their places. Some of them were watching from their boats, while others sat on blankets, on the sand. A handful climbed on top of the cabins, thinking they could get a better look.

James and Mary found a somewhat secluded area on top of a hill. They could still see the fireworks from where they were, but they just preferred to be alone. Mary spread out a very large blanket. She leaned back in James' arms. They didn't talk. For a while they just sat and watched the fireworks. It felt like a perfect moment. They kissed as Mary held on to James. This kiss was different, and James knew it. Mary turned around and looked deep into his eyes. James now knew that she was ready to take their relationship further. He certainly had not pressured her about sex, but he did wonder when and where it would happen. He had a sense that it was going to happen tonight. He was right.

Mary took off her sweater and her shoes. She grabbed James' shirt and pulled him towards her. He was shocked that she was the aggressor. But, he wasn't going to complain.

James took off his shirt and continuing kissing Mary. For a brief moment, they just stared at each other. They were young, and they were very much in love.

They helped each other remove the rest of their clothes. James was methodical. He put his right hand over her breasts. He touched her nipples. He had wondered what they felt like. She was massaging his neck and shoulders as he kissed her body. He was nervous, but very excited. Mary put her hands over his butt and rubbed his genitals.

It was very sensual. James made sure that he looked into Mary's eyes every so often. It was his way of showing Mary that he really loved her, and that he was interested in more than just sex.

For the first time, Mary and James made love.

Afterwards they sat back on the blanket. For a while they didn't say anything. They held hands, while looking at the stars. The fireworks were over, and they could hear many of the other kids jumping back on their boats, heading back to the other side. They knew they should be leaving soon too, but they wanted this moment to last.

Mary often thought about what it would be like her first time. Her family had a strong Christian faith. She was always taught that sex should wait until after marriage. She fully intended to follow that route. But, she never thought she would meet someone like Jimmy. She did not feel guilty. In her mind, James Evans was the first and last person she would ever make love to.

They eventually walked back to the cabins and headed home. James used a lantern in the canoe for some light. He paddled, and watched Mary as she looked at the sky. And he wondered how he got so lucky to meet someone like her.

CHAPTER 21

Football practice would be starting soon. From a purely competitive perspective, it couldn't come soon enough for James. It also couldn't come soon enough for Mary's father, who thought Mary was starting to get too serious with James. Quite frankly, Mary's mother shared some of those same concerns, but she really didn't push the issue. Mary's father figured James would be plenty busy with practice, and his job. Therefore, he reasoned that he and Mary would see less of each other.

Early August meant 10 days of intense football practice at Camp Notre Dame. At that time, just about every large high school put a lot of importance on their teams getting a couple hours away from home. The coaches wanted total concentration and focus from the players. The theory was that 10 days at camp would build camaraderie, unity and teamwork. What the coaches really wanted was to practice morning, noon and night without parental interference.

Before they would leave for camp, James, Stevie, Lenny and Jerry spent a Saturday at Lenny's camp. It was actually his grandfather's camp. Lenny got permission from his father to spend the day there. What he didn't realize was that Lenny's grandfather had several rifles still stored there.

The boys pulled out the .22's and the shotguns. They shot at fictional targets. They were dangerous, but at least they weren't drinking.

"So, let's hear about it, Jimbo," Stevie said.

"Hear what?"

"Come on – you've been dating Mary, how long now? When are we going to get some details?"

"I don't know what you're talking about," James tried to say innocently.

"Bull shit. Come on – have you guys done it or not?"

Lenny jumped in. "Now, now, he doesn't need to spill the beans."

"Thank you, Lenny," replied James.

"Jim, you can give me the details in private," Lenny noted.

All the while, Jerry stood there with a shotgun in his hand, nibbling on peanuts. At this particular moment, he was James' best friend, because he kept his mouth shut.

"When you guys getting married?" Steve continued to needle.

"When we do, I'll make sure you're the first to know," James said sarcastically.

"Hey, man, I'm not saying I don't dig Mary. I think she's great," Stevie advised. "I'm just saying – you really want to be tied down?"

"I don't feel like I'm tied down."

Stevie continued the inquisition. "Listen, do you guys talk on the phone every day?"

"Yeah...just about."

"Do you think about her all the time?"

"Yeah, I think about her a lot."

"You're tied down man. In fact, you're pussy whipped. We might as well start ordering our wedding tuxedos."

Jerry laughed. "That was a good one."

"Who the hell woke you up?" James said to Jerry.

"Face it, man, for all intents and purposes, you guys are already married," Stevie explained .

"Would you guys lay off? You're just jealous that Mary and I have something special."

"Ok, Hoss, whatever you say – Mr. Special," teased Stevie.

CHAPTER 22

When James and his teammates returned from football camp, it was as if he was returning from war. It might have only been 10 days, but to Mary it seemed like 10 years.

They quickly made up for lost time. James wanted to spend some quiet time with Mary. They went to Shepard's boat rental between Beaches 1 and 2.

"Jim! How are you there, young man?" Mr. Shepard shouted. "How's your mom?"

"Hi, Mr. Shepard, I'm doing okay. So is my mom."

"I haven't seen her in a while. We used to run into each other at Dolly's Bakery."

"Yeah, she still goes there from time to time. By the way, this is Mary."

"Nice to meet you, young lady," Mr. Shepard said, as he winked at James.

"Nice to meet you, sir," Mary said. She smiled – she saw his wink.

Mr. Shepard noted the color on James' face and neck. "Looks like you've been enjoying the sun."

James laughed. "Well, I don't know about enjoyment – just got back from football camp."

"Oh!"

"Yeah, we spent a lot of hours in the heat. I think I lost seven or eight pounds."

"I bet. I remember those days," Mr. Shepard said proudly. "How you guys looking? From what I'm hearing, everyone's saying you guys could make a serious run at States."

"Well, it's early," James noted. "But I think we're going to be tough to beat. We have a lot of guys back."

"Boy that would be something if WC could make it all the way to the title game. It's been a few years, hasn't it?"

"Ah, about five years. But we've gotten close the last couple years," James noted, as if to remind him they were still pretty good.

"Forgive me, I could talk football all day," Mr. Shepard said. "I know you kids didn't come here to listen to me. What can I do for you?"

"We were wondering if you had any paddle boats for rent?"

"Yep. Got a couple out back. Do you just want to rent it for a few hours?"

"Yes, sir. We will have it back around 2 o'clock," James said as he was pulling out his money.

"No, no – no, siree. Your money's no good here."

"I have to pay you something, Mr. Shepard."

"I'll tell you what. You guys go win yourselves a state championship this year, and we'll call it even."

"We'll see what we can do. Thanks very much, Mr. Shepard."

"Thank you sir," Mary said.

"Don't you mention it. Have fun now – just make sure you wear your life preservers."

James and Mary got the boat going and James started paddling slowly.

"Wow! Mr. Shepard really likes you – a free boat ride. Must be nice to be a West Cannon Lion."

James chuckled. "I am not sure it entirely has to do with football. Rumor had it that he always had a thing for my mother."

"Are you serious?"

"Oh, yeah. When I was younger, we seemed to run into him everywhere. I don't think it was always a coincidence. My mom used to talk to him so much- I just figured they may end up together."

James started rolling his neck back and forth. He stopped paddling.

"Hurts, huh?"

"When it tightens up, it hurts like hell. Some of the practices at camp were pretty physical."

"Turn around. Let me see if I can help."

James slowly turned around and sat back against Mary. She very lightly rubbed his shoulders and neck. Within minutes, James was starting to nod off. They let the boat drift very slowly.

Mary just held him. She didn't say anything. There was a slight breeze that seemed to mask some of the humidity. For Mary it was perfect. Although they had not known each other very long, and only recently became intimate, it was at this moment she thought that she and James could really be together forever. She didn't feel that way when she was alone. She constantly worried about which college James would attend. She worried that he would end up finding someone new – someone more interesting, more intelligent, and more worldly.

But it was at these moments when they were together that those worries seemed distant.

CHAPTER 23

Later that evening James and Mary drove to the other side of the Peninsula. They were at the furthest point northeast. James had heard that it was the most tranquil part of the beaches.

"We should have brought a large blanket. We weren't thinking," Mary said.

James went to the back trunk and opened it. "I might need some help carrying everything."

Mary had a confused look on her face. Then, she saw all the stuff in his trunk. "Oh my God, what is all this?"

"Just a little something I had planned." James took out a picnic basket and a large, old style foam coaler. He had a very large multi-colored blanket in the trunk.

They spread the blanket. "This is so romantic. You never stop surprising me."

"It's pretty cool, huh?"

"It's very cool."

James had deli sandwiches and potato chips at the bottom of the ice filled cooler. He opened the basket. He took out two wine glasses and a bottle of red wine.

"You are unbelievable."

"What? You can't have a picnic without wine."

"Where did you get the wine glasses? From home?"

"Yeah – we never use them. My mom will never know."

James poured them both wine. He held up his glass. "Well, a toast to the prettiest girl on this beach."

Mary held up her glass. "Right now, I'm the only girl on this beach," she said laughing.

"Please, don't ruin this moment. I've been working on this toast all day."

"With you, I wouldn't doubt it."

They ate and drank their wine. They watched calm waves come in. Every once in a while, seagulls would fly over. But, other than that, it was very peaceful.

"Hold on, I have to get something. Be right back," James said.

James came back carrying a guitar case.

"What is that?"

"What does it look like? It's my guitar."

"You play the guitar? You never told me that."

"Hey, there is so much more to me than just good looks, brains and football."

"Modesty apparently isn't one of them," she said, with a laugh.

"I've taken lessons for a few years." James took out the acoustic guitar from its case.

"Actually, Mary, I have been working on a song for you."

"For me?"

"Yeah, actually it's a lot harder than I thought to write a song."

James tuned it and started playing a slow song for Mary. It had a bit of country in it. He sang the words to her:

"Somewhere in the future,

She's waiting there for me;

All I want is a chance at love –

A chance for her to see.

If fate holds on tight,

And the angels hear my prayer,

We'll be together soon, my love;

We have a bond that's just so rare.

"I love you more and more each day, you see,

You make my whole life complete, you and me.

I love you more and more each day, you see,

You make my whole life complete, you and me."

"She changed my life, she filled my world,

She saw deep into my soul.

She opened my eyes to a brand new love,

When I'm with her, I lose control."

"I love you more and more each day, you see,

You make my whole life complete, you and me.

I love you more and more each day, you see,

You make my whole life complete, you and me."

James stopped and put down the guitar. "Well, that's what I have so far. I'm still working on it."

"I love it. I really do. Jimmy Evans, you are so talented for your age."

"You mean it? You really liked it?"

"I do! I've never been sung to before."

James put aside the cooler and basket. A breeze was starting to pick up. He held Mary, and wrapped the blanket around them. Mary would always say it was one of the most romantic nights in her life.

CHAPTER 24

The annual pep rally held the night before West Cannon's opening game was always one of the big highlights of the high school football season. This year it was even bigger, as the next day West Cannon would be facing Center Valley, one of their chief rivals. Usually this game would be scheduled for October, but the district's officials thought it would be fun to have these two teams play the opening week.

The rally included a large bon fire, WC's large marching band, the school's cheerleaders, hundreds of students and alumni, and an inspirational speech from their principal, Mr. William Hudson.

The rally was held in the back of the football field, where there was a lot of unused and un-kept farm land. The players were individually introduced to the stage – seniors first. The "stars" received the loudest ovations, and that included James Evans. As James stared out into the crowd, he noticed Mary standing to the left, on a hill. Mary waved. James smiled. Standing up there, Mary couldn't help but feel like she was starting to lose some control. Their magical summer had come to an end. Now, it was back to their respective schools. Their senior years would go fast. Would Jimmy be getting ready for a college football game this time next year – and where would that be?

James met up with Mary after the rally. "Hey, thanks for coming."

"I wanted to come."

"I won't tell any of your friends you were at West Cannon's annual rally."

Mary laughed. "I think they know I'd be here."

"Well, I'm glad you made it. I'm not real big on this rah-rah shit – I'd rather just play the game."

Mary didn't say anything.

"You okay?" James asked.

"I guess. I can't stop thinking about school next week."

"Yeah, I know what you mean. Summer just flew by."

Mary stepped closer to James and put her arms inside his Letterman's jacket. She held him close. It occurred to James that Mary was here to put a proper closure on summer.

She looked up at James. "I can't believe it's over – I don't want it to end," she said.

"It doesn't have to end." James tried to reassure her. But, he knew Mary was right.

"Promise me you'll stay with me forever, Jimmy."

"I promise."

"I mean it. Promise me nothing or nobody will keep us apart."

"Mary, I promise we'll always be together. You're not jealous, are you?"

"I am! I never was before, but then I never had a reason to be."

"What are you jealous of exactly?"

"Everything! Other girls..."

"Look at me. I am not interested in any other girls. I am only interested in you. You're the one I love. It's all going to be alright."

CHAPTER 25

PRESENT DAY – CHRISTMAS NIGHT

...Mary regained her thoughts.

"You left...you...just left."

"I know. I am so sorry. I was a young kid. I didn't realize then how much it would hurt you."

"You have no idea," Mary said loudly.

Mary paused. Tears were running down her face. "Do you realize the shame and embarrassment I brought to my family? It might be common in today's society, but you remember how it was back then. I was seen as an outcast in school, with my friends...with my own family!"

"I know. I know. I wasn't there when you gave it up. I remember struggling with what I should do."

"What the hell are you talking about? I didn't give up the baby."

"Huh? I don't understand. Your dad told me you were not keeping the baby."

"I ended up having a baby boy...a boy whose life you walked out on."

James couldn't comprehend everything. It was all too overwhelming.

"You had a boy?"

"Yes. A baby boy. I had Anthony. Anthony's your son. He's our son!"

CHAPTER 26

The clock was quickly turning on another Christmas. This one would be unique – to James...to Mary...to Anthony.

Mary went back to her room. There would be a lot more to say. But not tonight. Life-defining moments were not supposed to happen at their age.

James did not move from his chair. He was confused. He was scared. It was as if he was 18 years old again. It seemed like life was starting to repeat itself. *Now, being alone in a nursing home with no family hadn't seemed so bad*, James thought to himself. It was better than having to try to deal with all this.

James had a son. A son. A son he never knew about. He was angry at Mary's father. If he were alive today, James would probably kill him. How could he tell James that Mary was giving up the baby? What gave him the idea that he could play God? James thought about all the lives that were affected by Mary's father.

CHAPTER 27

James couldn't sleep that night. He might have dozed a few minutes here and there. But, that was the extent of it.

That morning, he asked Hannah to take him to the chapel. Hannah could tell James seemed disturbed. She didn't question him.

"I might be in here a while," James said, as she helped him into the chapel.

"No problem, Mr. Evans. I brought some paperwork with me. I will be right outside."

James was sitting in the front pew. A young man came out from behind the altar.

"Oh, I'm sorry, sir. I didn't know anyone was here."

"How are you, James?" the young man said.

"How did you know my name?"

"Pastor Jonah told me that a nice gentleman might stop by the chapel. I'm the Pastor's assistant. My name is Jose."

Jose looked very young. But he was very articulate and seemed to have a real sense of maturity about him.

"Actually, I'm not doing very well," James said.

"I'm sorry to hear that. Would you like to talk about it?"

"I'm really not sure where to even begin. It seems like everything I thought I knew had been wrong."

Jose sat down on a folding chair and listened.

"I think I may have made a horrendous decision. I should have let bygones be bygones."

"Hmmm. Do you think if you had let things be, you would have felt better about it?"

"I don't know. I don't know what to think."

Jose leaned forward in his chair and rubbed his chin with his hand. "So, this sounds like a "lesser of two evils" situation?"

"I guess you could say that."

"Well, I think you have to ask yourself whether the decisions you are making are having an impact on others."

"Lives have certainly been impacted," James noted. "I mean, maybe I should have just taken this to my grave. That way – no one gets hurt."

"I suppose you are right," Jose said. "But that would be the easy way, don't you think?"

"With all due respect, at my age, I don't need complications."

"I definitely understand that. But, I think regardless of age, or generation, trying to do what's right, even if it's painful, is still the best course of action."

James looked at Jose, and then looked at the cross. "How did you get to be so smart at such a young age?"

"Oh, I've been around. I'm older than I look."

Jose continued. "I think God challenges us, no matter our age. I guess what I am saying is that faith does not have an age limit. No matter how old you are, faith can be tested. We still are challenged to do the right thing – whether we are 18 or 80.

"Whoa, I'm nowhere near 80 yet," James said, trying to find some humor in this.

Jose laughed. "I know. I was just saying that rhetorically. I think that whatever you are struggling with – just trust in the Lord and do what you know is right."

"Hannah peeked in her head. "How's it going, Mr. Evans?"

"Ah, yeah, come on in."

Hannah leaned over and put her hand on James' shoulder. "You ready to go?"

"Yeah, I guess we should get back. James looked over at the altar and then to the side. He didn't see Jose. He wondered where he had gone.

"Can I get you something, Mr. Evans?" Hannah asked, as she noticed him looking around.

"No, I was just looking for Jose. He sure disappeared quickly."

"Jose?"

"Yeah, the pastor's helper. We were just talking."

"The pastor?"

"Yeah, I've talked to Pastor Jonah and Jose when I've come in here."

"Oh…oookay. Well, I don't see him," Hannah said.

"Sure hope to see him again," James said. "Sure is a bright young fella."

"I'm sure he is..."

CHAPTER 28

Shortly after Christmas Jennifer and Jacqui were busy cleaning Mary's house. They knew the chances of Mary returning home were extremely slim. The girls had a lot on their plates. They had to continually tend to Mary at Rosemont, but they also knew they had to continue working at Mary's house. The house needed to be completely cleaned, and eventually put on the market.

They were sorting through a lot of Mary's personal belongings. Jennifer was searching through some financial papers. "Jacqui, come here."

"What's up?"

"Did Mom ever mention another man to you?"

"What?" Jacquie abruptly asked.

"I was going through some old tax papers, and found these." Jennifer pulled out a stack of papers.

"What is that?"

"They're old letters Mom kept. They look like love letters."

Maybe we shouldn't be looking at these."

"Don't you want to know if Mom was seeing another man?'

"I can't believe we're even talking about this – Dad must be rolling over in his grave."

"Jacqui, aren't you even curious – what if Mom had someone else?"

"How do you know if they're from someone else? Maybe they're from Dad."

Jennifer took at closer look at one of the letters. "I don't think they're from Dad." She read the letter out loud:

My dearest Mary,

It's 10:15 p.m. Lights out was actually at 10:00. I'm writing this with a flashlight in my left hand.

The practices were really tough today. My entire body is sore. It seems like they put us through some extra hard practices. My body aches, but my heart aches more. (How's that for some poetry....) In all seriousness, I miss you so much. I never thought I would fall in love so soon. I'm just happy we met. I couldn't imagine my life without you.

Don't worry about the future. Everything will be okay. We will be together.

Well, I better turn off the flashlight before one of the coaches catches me.

Love always,

Your Jimmy

"Who's Jimmy?" Jacqui asked.

"I have no idea."

"Lights out? Was this guy in the military? I can't believe Mom would have an affair," Jacquie reassured herself.

Jennifer held her stomach. "Oh my God, I think I'm going to get sick."

Jacquie took the letter and read it. "Wait a minute! Look at the date on the letter – 8-13-60. Jennifer, Mom would have been what, 17, at that time? She still would have been in high school. This was way before she met Dad."

They collectively breathed a sigh of relief. They didn't really think Mary could ever cheat on their father. They didn't want to believe it.

But, as they both sat on the wooden floor next to their mom's cedar chest, they were wondering the same thing – who was Jimmy…and why did their mom keep these letters?

CHAPTER 29

Jacqui and Jennifer continued to work on their mom's house. Initially, they had decided they would no longer read any of the other letters.

That didn't last long.

"Jennifer!" Jacqui yelled.

Jennifer jumped. "Jesus, you scared the shit of me. What's up?"

"Did you see this before? You put all of Mom's jewelry in the upstairs bathroom, right?"

"Yeah – she didn't have that much, so I put it all together. I didn't get a chance to separate it yet."

"You didn't see this, then?"

"What is it?" Jennifer asked, as she entered the bathroom.

Jacqui held up the necklace with the half-heart, inscribed "My Jimmy."

"Oh my God," Jennifer said as she put her hands over her mouth.

"Just who Is this "Jimmy"?" Jennifer asked emphatically.

"Why would Mom keep this stuff?" Jacqui asked. "I mean, the only personal stuff we found from Dad was life insurance papers and the home designs."

"Jac, this "Jimmy" must have been Mom's first love. Geez, I don't remember keeping anything from my first love."

"Benny Robertson?" Jacquie laughed loudly. "You call that a first love? That was more like a science experiment."

"Be nice. He was kind of nerdy, I admit. But Benny gave me my first kiss."

"Kind of nerdy?" Jacqui quipped. "I'll never forget the look on Dad's face when you brought him home for the first time. I think dad questioned if he was actually a boy."

"Enough already about Bennie. What about this "Jimmy"?"

Jacqui thought about it for a moment. "Maybe we should take a look at just a few more letters – try to find out some more."

Jennifer agreed. They went back into Mary's bedroom, and pulled out the letters. They pulled out the first one:

7-5-60

My dearest Mary,

If last night was a dream I never want to wake up. It was the best night of my life. Thank you for sharing such a special moment.

It couldn't have been any better – it was a perfect end to a perfect day. I want you to be my first...and my last.

I woke up this morning feeling even closer to you. I didn't think that was even possible.

You are forever in my heart.

Love always,

Your Jimmy

Jennifer and Jacqui looked at each other. "Sharing such a special moment"? They didn't want to believe it, but they could figure it out.

They felt somewhat guilty reading these, but the curiosity was getting the better of them.

"Jennifer, look at this one – it's dated Thanksgiving 1960."

Thanksgiving 1960

My dearest Mary,

Happy Thanksgiving. We just finished eating. It's very quiet here.

I am just sitting here wondering what you are doing right now. I wish I were with you.

I noticed that a couple neighbors are outside putting Christmas lights on their houses. It has me in the holiday mood. I will see if my mom will let me start bringing up some of the decorations from the basement now, instead of waiting for December 1.

I was thinking what it would be like when we're older, and spend Christmas together. We'll be the first on our block to decorate the house. It'll be cool seeing our house all lit up when it's snowing outside. We'll have a lot of presents around our Christmas tree. And a lot of kids to open them! I can't wait.

Love always,

Your Jimmy

CHAPTER 30

At Rosemont it was evident that something was wrong with Mary. She had kept to herself at meal times, and in fact had been requesting to stay in her room, and have most meals brought to her.

On a Friday afternoon, Jennifer and Jacqui had met with one of the program directors, a nurse and physical therapist. Rosemont requested the meeting. Sarah Beninger was one of the program directors for new residents. She helped develop and coordinate programs covering the initial six months for new residents. At the end of each week, various representatives, including nurses, aides, therapists, and dieticians would provide input to Sarah. Those who worked closely with Mary were starting to become concerned.

"Thank you for meeting with us, especially on short notice," Sarah told the girls. "Why don't we quickly go around the room and introduce ourselves."

"I'm Gina Kensmith, one of the nurses who has been reviewing Mary's file."

"Hi, I'm Ron Bryant. We've met a couple times back when your mom first arrived."

"Oh, yes," Jacqui note. "We've seen you in that room across the hall."

"Yeah, I'm one of the physical therapists. I usually have Mary as one of my patients, although she does get other therapists. It all depends on who is scheduled."

Ron looked over to Delores Clayborn. Delores spoke with a real southern drawl. She was originally from Mississippi. "I'm Delores Clayborn. I work with the food service. We continuously monitor what the residents, especially the newer ones, are eating. We measure calorie intake and stuff."

After the introductions, Sarah took over. "Well, the reason we've asked you here was to provide you with an overall status as to how Mary's doing. It is our feeling that she is doing okay, but we do have some concerns, especially the past few weeks."

This was not totally unexpected as far as Jacqui and Jennifer were concerned. They were starting to see some definite changes in Mary, as well.

Sarah continued. "Why don't we start with you, Ron."

"Okay. Well, you've seen our physical therapy room. I mean, we call it physical therapy, but for most residents in this building, we really aren't trying to recapture something they lost. Rosemont does have a separate building where actual physical therapy takes place – where we're trying to rehabilitate someone. But just across the hall here, we may do some minor arm and leg strengthening exercises. For example, we have some residents see if they can pedal a bike tire with their arm or leg. We also have coordination exercise, such as tossing a beach ball to them, and seeing if they can catch it. Well, long story short, we have seen Mary's work in the therapy room fall off quite a bit. Please understand that we're not saying we are trying to get her to reach some new goals, or anything like that. But, quite frankly, it looks like the effort is no longer there. We know that she can actually do quite a bit physically – she's a strong person. But, lately she always seems to tell us she's tired or just doesn't want to do it. She's really not even trying much – at least not recently."

Jacqui and Jennifer nodded.

"Thanks, Ron," Sarah said. "Delores, how about you?"

"Well, from what I can tell Mary's appetite has not been good lately. It's not that she isn't eating at all, but she's definitely not eating nearly as much as she was. She's even refusing to eat any desserts. Her calorie count is certainly down. Early on, especially when Mary arrived, you could always count on her eating her desserts. She certainly was not picky in that regard."

Jennifer let out a smile. "Yeah, Mom was never a picky eater. There are not too many foods she doesn't like."

"Thanks, Delores. Gina, how about you?" Sarah said.

"Basically, I've been reviewing Mary's file, including her records when she arrived, and comparing them to this week. Although I'm not a psychologist, it is quite evident that Mary has withdrawn somewhat. We certainly don't expect any resident to be happy every day – that's not realistic. And although Mary is not the kind of person to always lead other residents in conversation, she typically does talk to others, whether it's at meals, or in the main living room. Recently she has seemed down, and rather aloof. I know some of the aides have noticed her staying in her room, and sleeping more."

Sarah interjected. "We certainly are not trying to frighten you. You know that we have a large staff who will always take a keen interest in all the residents. At this point we will monitor her very closely."

"We appreciate that," Jacqui said. "We share the same concerns. We'll do our best to try to get Mom to eat, and try to boost her spirits."

"It's difficult, I know," Sarah noted. "I know the residents don't like it when the staff continues to harp on them about eating. Whatever we can do to work together…"

CHAPTER 31

Mary was sitting in her room on a Thursday evening. Earlier in the week, there had been significant snowfall. It was very cold. The snow drifts covered Mary's window.

Jacqui visited earlier in the day. Because of the heavy snowfall, neither Jennifer nor Jacqui had been able to visit in a couple days. It didn't help that Rosemont was located on several hills, north of the city. That usually meant this area received more snow accumulation than other parts of the city.

These past few days provided a lot of time for Mary to think. She had not seen much of James, as he was having his meals sent to his room. She was trying to come to grips with everything. She was still upset – and rightly so. The fact is James left when he found out she was pregnant. At the same time, a strange rush of emotions had come back, that she hadn't felt in so many years. James was not just her first boyfriend. She was truly in love with him. It didn't matter how young they were then – she could not deny her feelings.

As she sat in her room, staring at the snow covered tree limbs, she couldn't help but wonder what would have happened if James had stayed? Would they have gotten married? Would she have lived the life she dreamed about when they were dating?

She felt incredibly guilty as she thought about this. After all, she did end up marrying a good man – a good provider. She grew to love her husband, and all that he stood for. She ended up having a comfortable, stable life.

But after finding out that Jimmy, "her Jimmy", was residing in the very next wing, it was as if the clock had been turned back.

The phone rang. Mary and her daughters had a secret code. When the phone rang, they would let it ring twice, and then hang up. Then, her daughters would call back. That way, Mary knew it was either Jennifer or Jacqui calling. Quite frankly, Mary didn't want to be stuck talking to her cousin, Edna. Any time Edna called, Mary was looking at a minimum 45 minute conversation. She didn't have the stamina, or the stomach, to listen to cousin Edna.

This time the phone rang continuously. Mary didn't answer. The phone rang again, and continued several times. The caller finally stopped. A few minutes later, the phone rang again. Mary was getting tired of listening to it, and picked it up.

"Mom?"

"Oh, Anthony, it's you. I thought it was someone else."

"You screening your calls?" Anthony joked.

"Actually, yes. Whenever cousin Edna calls, I can never get off the phone."

"Ah....got it. Sounds kind of mean to me..."

"You've never talked to Edna for an hour..."

"Ha ha. Good point."

Mary advised Anthony of her code with his sisters. They were now all on the same page.

"So, how are you doing, Mom?"

"Oh, I guess I'm doing okay."

"Jennifer had talked to me recently. She and Jacqui have had some concerns."

"Oh, do they?"

"Yeah, don't be mad at them. They're just worried. Are you feeling alright?"

"I'm alright. Nothing new."

"Nothing new?"

"No."

Anthony knew this wasn't going to be easy. But, he didn't think he would have to work to drag it out of her.

"Jennifer mentioned that you weren't feeling well, and maybe feeling a little down. I didn't know if you had been sick?"

"I'm not sick. I'm just tired. I've just been uncomfortable and uneasy."

Anthony took her literally. He had no idea she was referring to the situation with James.

"I don't pretend to know what it's like for you. But, I think you really have to give it a lot more time. I know you've heard that before."

Mary really didn't want to get into it. This was not the time or the venue to tell Anthony about his father.

She let out a long pause. "I don't mean to make everyone worry. I'll be fine, really. I'm just overwhelmed right now."

"Ok. I didn't mean to be a pain in the ass," replied Anthony.

"Oh, you're not a pain the ass...well maybe just a little..."

"I got that from you..."

They laughed. After hanging up, Mary wondered how Anthony would react when he found out about his father. Eventually they would both have to face the music...

CHAPTER 32

Jennifer and Jacqui decided to confront Mary about 'Jimmy'. After discussing whether they should even bring up the subject, they felt they had nothing to lose. Plus, they were nosey as hell. It also bothered them that their mom kept old love letters from someone other than their father.

It was Saturday. They took their mom to 5:00 mass at St. Patrick's church. Afterward they went to dinner at Red Lobster. Mary loved shrimp, and loved Red Lobster.

The weather was pretty decent for January. It was cold, but not frigid. It had not snowed in the last four days.

"Mom, we wanted to talk to you about something," Jacqui said.

"Yeah, it might not be any of our business, but it's been kind of bothering us," added Jennifer.

"What would you like to talk about, girls?"

They looked at each other, wondering who would go first. Jacqui took the lead.

"Mom, you know we've been cleaning your house."

"Yes, and I appreciate that very much. I know you girls have been very busy."

"Well, we've been going through some papers, trying to figure out what we need to keep," Jacqui said. "And we accidentally came upon some stuff."

"What's that, dear?"

Jacqui took a deep breath. "We came across some old letters."

The waitress came by their table. Mary ordered the shrimp, crab and lobster combination. The girls looked at each other. They were happy to see their mom order such a large meal.

"So you came across some papers?" Mary asked.

"Yeah, they were old love letters. We weren't sure whether you still wanted them."

Jennifer chimed in. "We're kind of embarrassed."

Mary didn't seem fazed at first, almost as if she didn't understand what Jennifer said.

Mom?"

"Yes, dear."

"When we went through some papers, we found old love letters," Jennifer repeated.

"You did?" Mary couldn't recall her husband writing letters. "I hope they weren't too embarrassing. You know I was young once."

Jennifer chuckled. She looked at Jacqui. At this point they realized their mom was right. Mary was human, and young once. She was no different than anyone else. On the other hand, it didn't answer their question about "Jimmy".

Jacqui took over the conversation. "Mom, it's probably none of our business, but we were curious about the letters. The letters were written by a "Jimmy".

Mary stopped eating. She said nothing.

"Do you remember a "Jimmy"? Jennifer asked.

Mary was deliberate in her response. "I remember Jimmy. He was my first love."

"We only read a few of them. There were quite a few letters," Jennifer noted. "At first, we thought they were from Dad."

"I don't think your dad was much of a letter writer. That wasn't his style."

"We were just surprised you would have kept some love letters from your teenage years," Jacqui said. "You probably forgot you had them. We figured you forgot to throw them out."

"I'd like to see them," Mary said.

Jennifer seemed surprised. "Really?"

"Yeah, I would like to take a look at them, if you don't mind."

"Sure – they're your letters, Mom."

CHAPTER 33

As requested, the next day Jacqui brought the letters to Mary. She dropped them off and helped get Mary ready for bed. She didn't stay. She knew her mom would want to look at them as soon as she could.

Mary sat up in her bed and turned on her night light. Jacqui had the letters tightly secured in an envelope. It took her a while to get the damn thing open. When she did, she couldn't believe it. The letters were in pretty good shape. A little bent. A little faded. But, after all this time, they looked pretty good.

She thought back about what it felt like to be a lovesick teenager ----- and the anticipation and excitement of receiving a letter from Jimmy.

She pulled one from the stack. It was dated September 6, 1960:

My dearest Mary,

Well, I'm sitting here in my last class of the day – English. I should be paying attention but it's hard to concentrate. The first day of senior year is not how I thought it would be. I wish it was still summer. I had the best time of my life – all because of you!

I'd better go. I got a feeling Mrs. Krause is going to call on me soon.

Love always,

Your Jimmy

Mary could just see him now. His head down - writing feverishly as if he were taking notes while Mrs. Krause lectured.

She remembered that Jimmy liked Mrs. Krause – because Mrs. Krause liked football. If the team had to leave early for a game, Mrs. Krause let them make up the work on their own time. Mrs. Krause was cool.

Mary selected another letter from the stack:

Late Friday Night, September 30, 1960

My dearest Mary,

It's 11:45 p.m. I am sore all over. That was a very physical game. My head is starting to feel a little better. At least the pounding has stopped. Coach Nichols was pissed after the game. After he was done screaming, he walked out of the locker room. I've got a feeling practice is going to be hell next week.

I could sleep all weekend. But, I have a lot of homework. We got slammed with math problems. I also have reports due next week for social studies and chemistry. It's going to be a long weekend.

I saw you at the game when we were coming out of the locker room. I'm glad you were able to make it. I always feel good when you are there. It means a lot to me.

Well, I should probably turn the light off, and hit the hay.

Love always,

Your Jimmy

More memories started rushing back to Mary. She didn't remember the letter specifically, but could recall that time. If her memory served her correctly, West Cannon lost that game. It was a brutal game, with a lot of fights breaking out.

She had looked forward to going to the games. Back then, the county stadium could easily hold 10,000 people for the big games. Mary would read in the newspapers that now a big game might fill 4,000 seats. *Nothing stays the same*, she thought. Back then, a big game at the stadium on a Friday night was the talk of the town.

Mary read through a few more letters. There were too many to go through at one time. Jimmy did not write very lengthy letters, but he certainly liked to write.

A thought dawned on her. She was reading letters from her first love, and he was in a room in the next wing. He was the father of her oldest child, a boy. This was reality. Yet, she couldn't help feel like she was caught inside a long dream.

Jayne Morrison came into her room. She was one of the aides who were often assigned to Mary. "Hey, Mary, you're up late."

"Oh, I'm just looking at some old stuff. I guess I lost track of time."

"That's okay. I can keep the night light on for you."

"No. I should really get some sleep. Can I ask you for a favor, honey?"

"Sure, Mary."

"Could you please put this somewhere safe?"

"Pretty important stuff, huh?"

"Yeah, they mean a lot."

"I'll tell you what, Mary. Why don't I put them in your lock box?"

"That's a good idea. Thank you, dear."

"Sweet dreams, Mary."

Jayne shut the light and closed the door part of the way. Mary noticed it was very quiet. She also realized something else. She told Jayne the letters were very important to her. And they were. She realized they were a link to her past, and would provide meaning to her future.

CHAPTER 34

There were counselors from Rosemont, as well as outside counselors Rosemont would contract with in unusual situations. This was one of those situations.

The setting was Rosemont's large executive conference room. Typically, it was used for executive strategy meetings. But Rosemont officials thought it would best to utilize this room for the meeting, especially because it was located away from the residence halls.

Dr. Dennis Philips was a lead psychologist. He had been a lecturer at colleges such as Penn State, Rutgers and Dartmouth. He was on the board of directors at Rosemont.

Anthony, Jacqui and Jennifer walked in with Mary. James was already there, seated at the end of the long table.

"Hello, everyone, I'm Dr. Dennis Philips."

Anthony and Dr. Philips shook hands. "Nice to meet you, Doctor."

"Please, call me Dennis."

Anthony noticed James at the end of the table. "Mr. Evans, how are you? I didn't expect to see you here."

"Hi, Anthony, it's nice to see you," was all James could say.

Jacqui and Jennifer acknowledged James. They looked puzzled as well.

Dr. Philips went through the various introductions. Dr. Peter Morgenstern was a professor of psychology, specializing in child psychology. Ruby Stein was one of the counselors at Rosemont, as was William Brady.

Dr. Philips started. "Thank you all for coming. Anthony, we understand you are in town for a few days. We would like to discuss a serious issue. At the start, we would ask that everyone keep an open mind. It won't be easy, but we encourage everyone to try to look at the big picture."

Jennifer and Jacqui still thought this meeting was about Mary's lack of eating and her recent, apparent depressed state. Anthony sensed there was much more to it.

"I'd like to turn things over to Mary."

Mary directed herself towards her children. "I wanted to talk to you about something.   As a family, I don't think we ever kept secrets from each other. I think we've always been open with each other."

Mary continued. "You know I loved your father very much. He was a good man. A stable man. We did have a good marriage." The room was very quiet. Mary took a long pause. "But, there has been another part of my life…" She had trouble finishing. She looked at Dr. Philips.

Dr. Philips intervened. "Basically, Mary thought it was important to talk about another part of her life. Things have come up recently that need to be addressed."

Anthony, Jacqui and Jennifer looked confused as ever.

Mary spoke up. "Thank you, Doctor. I think I'm okay now. You know family has always been the most important thing to me. That's why this is difficult to talk about.'

"Mom, just tell us what's on your mind," Jacqui said.

" I've loved two men in my life. Naturally, your father. But, before him I had loved someone very much. So much that I really thought I would end up with that person – my first love."

Jennifer cut in. "Jimmy?"

"Yes, dear – Jimmy." Mary collected her thoughts. "Well, coming here to Rosemont has brought back my past." She pointed to James. "This is Jimmy."

You could feel the wind let out of the room. There was stunned disbelief. James wasn't sure how to react, so he just kept his head down.

"When did you guys find out?" Jacqui asked. "How did you know?"

"At first I had no idea," Mary said.

"Neither did I," James said.

"We didn't discover it until recently," Mary noted.

"I don't know what to say, Mom," Jacqui said. "Wow..."

"How do you feel about it, Mr. Evans?" Jennifer asked.

"I was shocked. Your mom and I go way back. I...I just can't believe that after all these years we were reunited."

A quick look at Jennifer and Jacqui, and you could tell they felt "reunited" was a strange way to term this.

Dr. Philips jumped in. "It really is pretty incredible. In my work I have been involved in cases where people are reunited after many years. Obviously, this is a very unique situation. To have two people reunite in a situation like this is really amazing."

"I agree," Jennifer said. "How wonderful it is that you two can see each other again. What a great opportunity to get to know each other again."

"I second that," Anthony said. "It's like coming full circle. But, to be honest I am somewhat confused as to why the psychologists and counselors are here." He looked at Dr. Philips and Dr. Morgenstern. He put his hands up. "With all due respect…"

Dr. Philips laughed. Dr. Morgenstern gave a wide smile.

"We couldn't agree with you more, Anthony," Dr. Morgenstern said. "Normally, this wouldn't be a venue for people reuniting after many years." He then looked down and straightened his papers. He got a more serious tone. "But, there is more to this story. And after discussing with Mary, she has relayed to us that she would like to discuss this with all of you. She wanted her entire family here."

Dr. Morgenstern looked at Mary. "Mary, are you ready to tell your story?"

Mary smiled, as she pushed her glasses up further. She looked at her children. "I want to tell you all something. At first, I wasn't sure if I should say anything. But, as I said we always made it a point not to keep secrets from each other."

Mary turned to James. "It's true about Mr. Evans and me. James was my first love. And we were very much in love. I can honestly say that I thought we were going to get married."

Mary reached for the pitcher of water. Dr. Morgenstern jumped in and poured her a glass. Mary took a sip. She contemplated what she was going to say next.

She looked at James. "When Mr. Evans and I were dating, it got pretty serious very quickly. We loved each other so much. I was brought up under a strict Christian faith. I had intended to follow that with regard to relationships. But when I fell in love with Mr. Evans, I began to look at things differently. We knew it was right between us."

You could hear a pin drop.

"I got pregnant at that time, when I was 18. I kept my baby. I kept my Anthony." She looked at James. "Our Anthony."

CHAPTER 35

Jennifer and Jacqui left the room. They didn't have to be asked. They knew this was a time for Anthony and his mother...and father.

The counselors stayed in the room. Anthony had not said anything. His biological father might have been in the same room, but he was still a stranger to Anthony. He was now beginning to wonder how well he knew his mother.

Dr. Morgenstern saw this as an opportunity to intervene. "Anthony, I know this is very overwhelming. I've specialized in cases where children are reunited with a parent they had never known. I would like to extend any assistance and services that we may be able to offer. Our organization has many full time counselors. They are very qualified and experienced."

Anthony looked down, and then looked at Dr. Morgenstern. He only nodded. "I'd like to talk to my mother and Mr. Evans alone, please."

"Absolutely," Dr. Morgenstern said.

Mary tried to look at Anthony. She felt ashamed.

"I'm sorry, Anthony," Mary said. "I should have told you long ago."

"Wow!" "You should have told me long ago? That's the understatement of the year!"

Mary felt sick. She knew it was right to tell him, but this was going to be one of the most difficult issues to deal with.

"All these years, you told me my father had run out on us...that you had lost touch completely - but that he had died years ago."

"I did leave – I ran out," James spoke up. "I hadn't kept my promise. And my life was never the same."

Mary looked at James. For the first time she could see the pain in James' face. Up until now, she really hadn't thought about how all of this affected James.

"Why did you leave my mother? How could you have done that?"

"I don't know. I don't know. I was young and scared. I made some huge mistakes."

Anthony sat back in his chair and just stared at James, in disbelief.

"Did you even try to look for me? Did you ever try to get in touch with my mom?"

James knew some of the reasons he had left, but this wasn't the time. There was enough to deal with right now.

"I am so sorry, Anthony," Mary said. "I know I've hurt you. I wish there was something I could say."

Anthony let out a sarcastic chuckle. "You don't know what to say? I just found out my biological father is in the same assisted living center as my mother. What if we had chosen another nursing home? Had that even occurred to you?"

Anthony ran his hands through his hair. "I have to go. I have to get out of here."

There was nothing Mary or James could say that would make things any better.

Anthony's comment hit James hard. Mary had apparently told Anthony that his biological father had died. James thought about it some more. He guessed it made sense. By telling him his real father had died probably helped put some closure in Anthony's life. James figured he might have done the same thing if he had been in Mary's shoes.

But, now - so much for closure.

CHAPTER 36

Jacqui and Jennifer saw Anthony leave. They helped Mary back to her room. The aides had already taken James back to his room.

There was little said. The girls assisted Mary to the bathroom and then to her bed. It was early but she wanted to lie down. A couple of the nurses came in to see if Mary needed anything. Jacqui had some errands to run but Jennifer stayed. As Mary started falling asleep, Jennifer sat in the rocking chair next to her bed. *We've always been a pretty close family,* Jennifer thought. Even though Anthony lived out of town, he usually made it a point to keep in contact often. He was there when the family needed him. Now, they would have to be there for him.

Mary slept for a while, and Jennifer fell asleep in the chair. It was eerily quiet, as if the residents of Rosemont knew to be especially quiet that night.

"Aren't you uncomfortable, honey?"

"No, I'm okay, Mom."

Mary grabbed Jennifer's hand. Jennifer realized this was not the time to ask questions. Her mom just needed her to be there for her right now.

"How long have I been asleep?"

Jennifer looked at her phone. "Oh, my, it's late. You've been asleep for over two hours."

"I think I needed it."

"I think you did, too."

"Oh, what have I done? I am sorry to put you kids through this."

"Hey, we'll get through this, including Anthony. You'll see."

"I certainly hope so. I really hurt your brother."

"Things will work out – you'll see," Jennifer said in a hopeful tone.

"Thank you, honey."

"It sounds like you and James were really in love."

"We really were." Mary then started to laugh to herself.

"What's so funny?" Jennifer asked as she squeezed her mom's hand.

"Oh, I was thinking back to homecoming week in our senior year. We almost ended up not going – all because of my jealousy.

"Tell me about it."

"Well, if I recall, I think it all started a few weeks before the homecoming dance…"

CHAPTER 37

...October, 1960

"Hey, James...good luck."

"Thanks, Catherine."

Catherine Yoder was one of West Cannon's cheerleaders. She was cute. She was outgoing. And she had a reputation.

James had heard about her reputation. He wasn't certain what to believe. He knew one thing. Mary did not like her. She knew Catherine was a flirt. She had heard that Catherine liked James as more than just friends.

James and his West Cannon teammates had left their locker room and were headed to the field. On this Friday evening, WC was playing host to the Allegheny Eagles. They were a very solid team, and a good test for West Cannon.

On the first series, James intercepted a pass and returned it for a touchdown. The crowd erupted. West Cannon's cheerleaders were standing in the end zone where James scored. Catherine virtually jumped on James' back. She thought it was funny. Mary – not so much.

West Cannon went on to win big that night. It really wasn't a contest, to the surprise of many. It was considered a big win for WC, if only because of the way they dominated. The team gathered at mid-field right as the game ended. Many of the student body stormed on to the field. Mary stood watching from the stands. She was clapping – maybe not for WC, but certainly for James.

Mary could see the cheerleaders circling the players. Naturally, Catherine was able to work her way up to James. She could see them hugging. Interestingly, she didn't see Catherine hug any other player.

"Let's go," Mary demanded.

"Aren't you going to stay around and see James?" asked Marie Johannson. Marie and Veronica Mayer were friends of Mary, who also attended Crestfield.

Veronica cleared her throat, as if to give Marie a signal. Marie caught on. She saw Catherine hanging on James.

"Don't worry about it, Mary," Veronica said. "She's just a tramp. Everybody knows it."

"Yeah, but she's had her eyes for Jimmy, and she gets what she wants, from what I hear."

The girls left. After the team showered and changed, James headed out to see Mary. It was something they had done since opening game. Regardless of the outcome of the game, James could always count on seeing Mary outside the locker room. Because James' mom often worked two jobs, she was rarely able to see James play. So, he really looked forward to seeing Mary after the home games. It was comforting to him.

He didn't realize at first why she was not there on this night. He would soon find out.

CHAPTER 38

"Good morning – God, you look horrible," Drew Stanton told James.

Drew arrived early the next morning. They had planned to go fishing on the west pier. Drew was one of West Cannon's wide receivers. He caught a touchdown pass the previous night.

"What time is it?"

"It's 7:00, Jimbo. C'mon, before all the fish are caught."

"Oh, man, I'm exhausted. Come on in. Give me a minute to get ready."

"OK, man, but not too long," Drew said, still concerned about the fish.

The boys got in Drew's truck and headed to the pier. A stop at McDonald's drive thru was a must.

"Nice, cool morning. The waves are moving. Should be good for fishing." Drew was an excellent fisherman.

"How is it that you are so fuckin' cheerful, so early?"

"I'm always this way when I don't have to go to school."

"I lost track of you last night," James said. "Where'd you go after the game?"

"Me, Johnny and Mike went over to Chico's house. We kind of tapped into Chico's dad's beer."

"Kind of?"

"Ok, we found it in his cellar. Do you know they have a second fridge in their cellar? It's wild."

"They have another fridge in the cellar? What the hell for?"

"I don't know. But, that's where the old man's beer was. Hopefully, he doesn't count cans."

James laughed. "I never thought of that. When did you get home?"

"I didn't. I went to your house, from Chico's."

"Jesus. Don't your parents wonder where you are at?"

"Nah. Hell, as long as we win, and I make some big plays, my dad doesn't say too much. He knows my only ticket to college is through football."

"Have you heard from any other schools?"

"Just got some letters from Ohio State and West Virginia."

"Cool."

"What about you, Jimbo?"

"Illinois sent a letter of interest to school last week."

"Illinois? Shit, I didn't know anyone from Illinois was scouting our games."

"Yeah, I hadn't really thought about going that far away. I just wish we could enjoy the season and not worry about that shit."

Drew smiled. "It looked like you were enjoying the celebration after the game."

"What do you mean?"

"What do I mean? Catherine."

"Ah, she was just jumping around. She's just a friend."

"Jimbo, either you're naïve as hell, or you're just playing dumb. She does not want to be your "friend"."

"You're crazy, man."

"Let me put it this way...Oh, shit, wait...I got something." Drew pulled back, and reeled in the line. He kept at it. "Ah, look at that fucker – a beautiful perch." As quickly as Drew caught it, he tossed it back in the water.

"What were we talking about?" asked Drew. "Oh, yeah, Catherine. You know she wants you."

"We're just friends. She's always acted like that."

Drew looked at James. "Really? I don't have any female friends that hug me and hang on me all the time. I'd like to have a friend like that."

"Yeah, I mean, she's affectionate. But that doesn't mean I'm going to do anything."

"Well", Drew said as he caught another fish, "most guys in your situation would look at it differently. They'd be all over her. In fact, from what I hear, a lot of guys have been."

"I think that's just her reputation. I think she tries to live up to that. But, she's not like that all the time."

"You think it's an act, do you, Jimbo?"

"I just think she has self-esteem issues, and she tries to act differently than she really is."

"Holy shit! And I thought you were going to study architecture in college. Hell, you should be our team psychologist."

"Ha Ha, very funny. And by the way, why the hell are you catching all the fish?"

"Reel in your line, Jimbo."

James reeled in his line.

Drew gave James a disgusted look. "Just as I thought – your bait fell off."

"Shit. Wasn't paying attention. You got me all wound up."

"Hey, we'd all like to have an old fashioned, nice girlfriend, and another wild chick on the side who wants you. I wish I had your problems."

"You're nuts. Ain't nothing going on. Mary and I are good. I don't think of Catherine that way."

"Ok, Jimbo, whatever you say," Drew said, as he reeled in another fish. He continued to toss them back.

"Why do you keep throwing them back? That could be our supper."

"Shit. We ain't having fish, Jimbo. If anything, you're taking me out for dinner. I need to hear more of your psychoanalysis. I'm impressed."

"I'm taking you out to dinner?" asked James.

"Yeah – and thanks, by the way."

CHAPTER 39

James got home late Saturday. He called Mary, but her dad said she wasn't home. He called again and received the same message from her mother. *Her mom sounded apprehensive though,* James thought. If there was one thing James could rely on, it was his instincts – even at such a young age. His instincts told him Mary was home – and that she was pissed.

James tried calling again Sunday, but there was no answer.

There was a buzz Monday at West Cannon. There was an energy. WC had just won a big game. The school year was well underway. James and his classmates were finally starting to feel like seniors.

The Student Government was starting to promote the upcoming homecoming game and dance. It was just two weeks away. The game with Lewistown would be played on a Friday, with the dance the following evening. And because James had been nominated for homecoming king, he and his date would be introduced, along with the other nominees, during halftime of the game. The last time he checked, he had a ticked off girlfriend. He'd look awfully stupid all alone during the introductions.

James' sixth period class was advanced mathematical concepts. He loved math. He sat next to John Langdon, who was one of West Cannon's defensive linemen.

"Hey, man, practice shouldn't be too bad today, you know," John said.

"Are you kidding me, John? The coaches will probably put us through hell today. They'll want to make sure we don't get complacent."

"Shit. I didn't think of that. I was looking forward to an easy practice."

"Can you recall any "easy" practices with Coach Nichols?"

"Point well taken, Jim. Hey what's up with you and Mary?"

"What do you mean?"

"I was over at Matt's house yesterday. He heard that you and Mary weren't speaking to each other. You guys have a fight or something?"

"Apparently she's mad at me. She won't return my calls."

"You know women!"

"I know that I don't know them," Jim noted.

CHAPTER 40

My Dearest Mary,

I've been trying to call you. I would just like to talk. I don't know what I did wrong, but whatever it is, I apologize.

I miss talking to you. I missed seeing you after the game last Friday. I always look forward to that.

I was wondering if we were still going to the homecoming dance. I hope so! I don't want to pressure you, but I was definitely looking forward to it.

I'd really like to hear from you. I'd like to know what I did wrong.

Love always,

Your Jimmy

As with many of his letters, James stuck it in the opening of Mary's locker. Her locker was on the first floor of the main entrance to Crestfield. It didn't matter that James didn't go to that school. At that time, you could walk freely in and out of schools.

With some of his other letters, he might give it to one of Mary's friends to give to her. He was confident that none of her friends would read them.

If he was daring he would climb the lattice on the side of Mary's house. Then, he would lean over to her bedroom window, open the screen, and throw the letter in. He did that a couple times. It was hell on his back, and she often would be in her room. He always liked to surprise her with his letters.

Several days passed and James had not heard from Mary. He went from confused, to worried. This was the longest stretch that they had not talked. For all intents and purposes this was their first fight.

West Cannon was on the road that weekend, playing Annville Heights. Annville was a small school, and as expected, WC kicked their asses. It was almost anti-climatic after the previous week's win.

It was a 2 ½ hour bus ride back to West Cannon. James sat at the back of the bus. George Stueben sat across from him. George was an interesting character. He didn't start and didn't play much. But, he got to play a lot today as WC pulled most of their starters at half. He liked football, but didn't love it. He was gifted musically and artistically. James thought he played football just to try to prove to everyone he wasn't different.

"You got to play a lot today, George."

"Yeah, I was ready. I figured we'd be kicking the crap out of them by halftime."

"You played pretty good out there."

"Thanks, Jim."

"What are you doing this weekend?"

"Well, I gotta finish a research paper for Scully's class. He's a pain in the ass with all those research papers."

"I'm glad I don't have him," James said, thankfully.

"Be thankful. The guy thinks his class is the most important thing in our lives."

"They all feel that way."

"I'm still going to Shooter's party tomorrow night. I'm not missing that. You going?"

"Yeah, I was planning on going. I have some homework myself."

Shooter wasn't on the football team. He was one of the senior class clowns, and popular. He got his nickname because he once accidentally shot himself in the leg at a firing range. He always told people he couldn't play football because of the injury. The fact was -- he stunk at football. Apparently he wasn't very good with a rifle, either.

CHAPTER 41

Shooter's house was interesting. He was a cowboy, or at least his father was. There were many rifles and pistols hanging on the walls. *Hopefully, they weren't loaded,* James thought to himself.

"Gentlemen, thank you for coming," Shooter said, coming in from the back porch, James, Stevie, Lenny and Jerry came to the party together.

"Where were you?" James asked.

"I was feeding the horses. I almost forgot to. My father would have kicked my ass if I forgot."

"Where is your old man?" asked Stevie, never one to mince words.

"My parents went to Louisville. They aren't coming back until Tuesday. They said I wasn't allowed to have friends over."

"I see you gave that a lot of thought." James said.

"Well, I have a couple days to clean up, so what the hell." Shooter patted Lenny on the back. "Enjoy the party, boys."

As Shooter tended to other guests, Stevie looked around the room. "Christ, I feel like the Indians should be invading soon. Nice house", he said sarcastically. "Let's grab some beers."

Shooter was a planner, if nothing else. He put all of his father's beer away. He had some "friends" get him some new cases of beer. The boys knew better than to ask when or where he got it. Tomorrow, Shooter would put back his dad's beer in the fridge. Pure genius.

It was a decent party. Nothing being broken that James could tell. But there were a lot of people. Some of them were playing pool in the basement – an 8-ball tournament. There were others sitting outside on the large back porch. One of the advantages of living on a large farm was that there were no neighbors close by. No neighbors to tell Shooter's parents.

James was sitting in the living room. This was the first time he felt relaxed in several days. That feeling didn't last. Mary walked in with her quartet of Hearts. There was something different about her. James noticed it right away. She would typically wear a little makeup, but not much. Tonight, she had lipstick and heavy eyeliner. Her hair looked like it had come in contact with an electrical outlet. She was wearing high heels. *What was this about?,* James wondered.

James noticed that some of the guys stopped what they were doing, and were staring at her. For the first time, James felt jealous - and very vulnerable.

Stevie walked over to James. "Damn, man, can I ask your girlfriend out?"

"Ha ha. Very funny."

"I've never seen her like that, man."

"That makes two of us, Stevie." James put down his beer and walked over to Mary.

"Hey."

"Hey," Mary replied.

"I've been trying to call you."

"Yeah. I've been busy."

James just looked at her and nodded his head. "I didn't expect to see you here."

"You think you're the only one who goes to parties?"

James was startled. What in the hell was going on? "No, I just didn't expect to see you. It's a nice surprise."

You could tell Mary wanted to shoot back but that was not her personality. So, she said nothing. She and the girls joined the party, leaving James standing alone at the front door.

CHAPTER 41

The next day James drove by Shooter's house to see if he needed help cleaning up. That wasn't the real reason, but that's what he would tell Shooter. James did not stay very long at the party and he really wanted to know what happened with Mary after he left.

"Dude, what's up?" Shooter was picking up trash on the front lawn.

"Hey, Shooter, just wanted to see if you needed some help."

"Hell, yeah. Thanks. There are garbage bags in the garage."

"You've been at this for a while?"

"No, hell, I just got up about a half-hour ago."

"Shooter, it's 1:30 in the afternoon."

"I know. I never got to bed until about 8:00 this morning. I just started cleaning. I figured I'd start with the outside first. That's probably the easiest."

He wasn't kidding. After quickly finishing they went inside.

"Good God, Shooter. It looks like a war zone."

"Yeah," Shooter replied, with a smile. Apparently, hosting a major party was more important to Shooter than worrying about the consequences.

There were beer and wine bottles everywhere. There were cigarette butts everywhere.

"Shooter, it smells like a bar."

"Yeah, we'll have to do something about that."

James just looked at Shooter.

They grabbed a bunch of garbage bags and got to work.

"I really appreciate this, man."

"No problem. Sorry I didn't stay longer last night."

"Yeah, I noticed you didn't stick around too long."

"Wasn't feeling great, I guess." James had to ask. "Did Mary stay?"

Shooter stopped throwing bottles in the bag. He looked out the window, as if he vaguely remembered last night.

"If I recall, she stayed for a while. You guys broke up?"

"No. Why?"

"Well, she was dancing with some other guys...I just figured."

"What guys?"

"I don't know, man."

"Sorry, didn't mean to snap."

"It's okay. I don't know what guys. You know, she and her friends were dancing in groups."

"She wasn't slow dancing with anyone?"

"I don't know, man -she might have been..."

James suddenly felt like he had been sucker punched.

Shooter looked over at him. He felt sorry for James. "I did see her dancing with someone. I didn't want to be stool pigeon."

"I know."

"Hey, it seemed like everyone at the party was dancing. I'm sure it's no big deal."

James knew Shooter was trying to be reassuring. He had always known Shooter to be crazy and somewhat irresponsible. In this instance, he knew him to be a good friend.

James and Shooter cleaned the entire house. James did not say much. He could not imagine Mary slow dancing with another guy. The more he thought about it, the harder he worked. At least it helped Shooter.

CHAPTER 42

HOMECOMING WEEK AT WEST CANNON

MONDAY

It was not your typical Monday morning. The Student Government had worked over the weekend, putting up more decorations and banners.

The Homecoming game was Friday night, with the dance the following evening. The halftime festivities and the dance were always something to look forward to. However, the current circumstances left James very confused. Would Mary still be his escort to the dance? Were they even still together?

WEDNESDAY

Two days had passed, and not a word from Mary. James was actually wondering if he should be asking someone else to be his escort for this weekend. He admitted to himself that he didn't want to look like an idiot without an escort on Friday night.

Practice that day was nasty. The weather was cold and rainy. Some of the guys didn't feel like practicing in those conditions – which gave the coaches even more reason to yell.

"Evans, do you need an invitation to get to the receiver?" Coach Carlson yelled. "How about you get your head out of your ass and start playing some football."

Carlson always had a way with words, but James knew he was right. This was a big game, and he needed to take it a little more seriously. He decided that for the rest of the week, he would concentrate on the game. If Mary showed up Friday, fine. If not, oh well...

FRIDAY

Homecoming Game, 1960

The Lewistown Beavers were a solid team. There was a philosophy that says a school should not schedule a good team for its homecoming game. The theory was that you should try to schedule an "easier" team, so that your chances of winning your homecoming game increased. When this game was scheduled right after last season, Lewistown had come off a losing season. What West Cannon didn't foresee was that the counties around Lewistown would be re-districted.   That meant that several players from nearby Jamesport were permitted to play for Lewistown this year. It instantly made Lewistown a stronger team.

West Cannon arrived very early to their stadium. On one side of the school, there were several classrooms that overlooked the north end zone. James decided to go up to one of the classrooms. He just wanted to be alone for a while before the game. He sat back and watched the band going through their routines in preparation for half time.

He looked over at the other side of the field, and could see several girls coming out of the other locker room. They had dresses on. He looked closer. He could make out what looked like Mary. It was her! He got excited. He instantly could feel the butterflies in his stomach. As the week went on, he started to doubt that she would come. James started thinking about halftime again. How awkward would this be?

James watched the girls. He immediately noticed that they seemed to be getting along. They were helping each other with their makeup. For some reason, he felt reassured that this was just a friendly competition. Initially, James was not excited about being nominated. He was usually low-key and didn't like to be put on display in front of other people. That feeling changed when he saw how excited Mary was when he asked her to homecoming.

"Hey, you okay, Jim?" Coach Murphy asked. "I didn't know anyone was up here."

Coach Murphy was WC's defensive coach.

"Yeah, everything's okay, coach. I was just getting away from everyone – thinking about the game. Should be a good one."

"I think we're ready."

"We're ready, coach!"

"You nervous?"

"Nah – just excited. Once I get that first hit in, things start to calm down."

"No, I was talking about half time."

James looked surprised. "Coach, I didn't know you were up on that stuff."

"I heard you were nominated, Jim. I have my sources."

"Don't worry, coach. My mind is on the game."

"I'm not worried about that. We never have to worry about you when it's time to kick it off. But, you should enjoy this. You'll see – it's a big event in your life."

Coach Murphy sat on top of one of the desks. He gazed out to the field. He had a certain look in his eyes. You could tell he was reminiscing.

"I remember my homecoming game. I was a senior at Akron High School."

"Ohio?"

"Yep. I'm originally from Ohio. I went to college in Pennsylvania, and never left. Anyways, we played Warren Central that night. I don't remember too much of the game, but I'll never forget halftime. Like you, I was nominated for Homecoming King."

"You?"

"Yeah, me! I was quite the "looker" back then."

James laughed. "I didn't mean it like that."

"I know. I'll tell you, it was a lot of fun. I felt like I was on top of the world. I can remember it like yesterday. She was beautiful."

"Did you win?"

"No, we were runner-up. Finished second to Harvey Feingold."

"Oh, sorry to hear that."

"No, no. I got the last laugh."

"What do you mean?"

"Harvey ended up embezzling from a company he worked for. Spent quite a bit of time in prison, I'm told."

"Wow."

Coach Murphy got up and slapped James on the back. "Well, better get ready – we've got a game to play."

"OK, Coach. Hey, coach."

Coach Murphy turned around. "Yeah?"

"Whatever happened to your date that night?"

"I married her. I guess you could say I ended up finishing first…"

CHAPTER 43

As expected, the game with Lewistown was a battle. What wasn't expected was how flat West Cannon came out of the locker room. It was a horrible first quarter – four penalties and a fumble. WC found themselves down early, 17-7. They settled down in the second quarter, and got within three points at halftime.

James and a couple teammates stayed on the field as the rest of the team headed to the locker room. The Homecoming Queen nominees walked through a giant heart-shaped figure, loaded with balloons. One at a time, they would walk through and meet their date. They would then proceed to stand on the riser. This was the first time James saw Mary close up in her dress. She was beautiful. Her hair was up, and it looked like she had some sparkles in it. She didn't have much makeup on – certainly not what she looked like at Shooter's party. She had natural beauty. She didn't need much makeup.

As she approached, James held out his arm. They walked up to the riser and looked into the crowd.

There were 12 couples standing on the riser.

'I didn't know if you were coming."

" I agreed to come – I made a commitment," Mary noted.

"Well, I'm glad you're here."

"Of course you are – you'd look stupid standing up here alone."

James laughed out loud. He had been thinking the same thing. Mary made a crooked smile. It was the first positive sign in the last two weeks.

"Sorry I'm so sweaty."

"You should be. You've been on the field a lot."

James was impressed. Their defense had been on the field a lot. It proved that Mary was watching him.

"You look very pretty. That's a really nice dress."

"Thank you."

James felt better that they were at least having somewhat of a conversation.

Each couple was introduced. James and Mary received some of the loudest cheers. There were a couple quick speeches by the Principal and the Student Government President. In the end, James and Mary finished runner-up. Roger Bender and Lisa Grimes were crowned 1960 Homecoming King and Queen.

Both James and Mary felt very proud...and relieved.

"Well, second place is not bad," James said.

"Nope. Nothing wrong with that."

"I have a feeling I'll end up finishing first," James said, in reference to his conversation with Coach Murphy. Mary just gave him a strange look.

"Well, I better get up to the locker room."

"Yeah, good luck in the second half."

"Thanks. I'll call you tomorrow."

"Alright," Mary responded, almost nonchalantly.

James started walking back to the locker room. He was trying to look at things positively. At least he and Mary talked – albeit, it wasn't deep conversation. He couldn't dwell on that now. He had a second half to play.

As James made it to the top of the steps, he saw Coach Murphy standing outside of the locker room, smoking a cigarette. He winked at James. They both knew what each other was thinking.

CHAPTER 44

James picked up Mary the next evening. There was no need to go to dinner, as the school was hosting a variety of finger foods, snacks and drinks.

"Hello, James."

"Hello," he said to Mary's mom.

"Congratulations on the game last night."

"Thank you."

West Cannon had a big second half and earned a solid victory over Lewistown.

Mary came down her staircase. If it was possible, she looked even more beautiful than the night before. She had on the same dress, but she wore a shawl. She wore a necklace with a cross that had the shape of a clover. She also had on a glaring diamond bracelet.

"Hey, you look really pretty."

Mary looked down and straightened her dress. "Thanks."

"Well, you ready?"

"Sure." Mary gave her mom a hug.

James noticed that her father did not come in from their dining room. He could hear the calculator buzzing. *Maybe he was working on his finances*, James thought. He was just glad he stayed in the dining room. It's uncomfortable when he's in the same house with James, let alone the same room.

The dance was held in West Cannon's gymnasium. The Student Government did just as good a job with the gymnasium, as they did with the school halls and cafeteria. It was very festive.

And with Halloween not too far off, several Halloween decorations were included.

James and Mary met up with Stevie, Lenny and Jerry, and their dates. The rest of the Queen of Hearts also arrived with their dates. They moved a few tables together.

"Would you like a drink?" James asked Mary.

"Sure."

Stevie hit James in the arm. "I'll go with you."

"I didn't know you liked punch that much, Stevie."

"I don't – I hate the stuff. You know I'm a beer guy. Hey, don't look behind you, but your other girl's here."

James started to turn.

"No, man, don't turn around."

"Who's here?"

"Catherine...and she's looking over here. How are you gonna play this one, Hoss?"

"What do you mean?" James asked, as he kept pouring more cups of punch.

Stevie took the punch ladle from James. "First off, are you pouring cups for the entire senior class? Twenty is enough – don't you think?"

"Sorry, guess I'm a little nervous."

"No shit. Second, as I see it, you've got a choice. You can go over to her now and say hi, or have her staring at you all night."

"What's the third option?"

"There is no third option."

"I didn't think she'd be here."

"Why? Where's there's a penis, you can usually find Catherine."

"That's real nice, man," James said. He then smiled and let out a laugh.

"That was a good one, wasn't it?" Stevie said proudly.

"Let's just go back to the table."

The girls sat at the tables and drank their punch. James stood over Mary, next to her chair. He kept looking around, keeping an eye on Catherine.

After several rock n' roll songs, the band played their first slow song.

"Would you like to dance?" James asked Mary.

"Um…alright."

They started dancing, although James noticed Mary was not entirely close. She was looking around. James wasn't sure if he should say something at this moment. Nothing came to mind, anyways.

Within minutes, Catherine came over.

"Hey, cut in time," she said, as she took hold of James' arm.

Mary and James were both stunned. Before they knew it, Catherine had her arms around James' neck.

Mary didn't know whether to throw a punch, or throw a fit. She was too embarrassed to do either. She quickly walked back to the table.

James tried to remain calm. He looked over to Mary a few times. It seemed like the damn song would never end. When it was over, Catherine squeezed him tight and gave him a kiss. He went from feeling uncomfortable to feeling somewhat violated. He genuinely liked Catherine, but maybe his friends were right. She seemed to be taking liberties.

When he got back to the table, he could tell Mary was upset. She looked like she was trying everything she could to hold back the tears.

She remained quiet. Her friends didn't.

"I can't believe that tramp cut in like that, "Rhonda Sue spoke up.

"Rhonda Sue..." Mary tried cutting in.

"No, Mary, that bitch needs to be taught a lesson."

Stevie came back to the table. "Hey, what'd I miss?" Stevie knew darn well what had happened. He was smiling.

"Do you want to go to the rest room?" Mary asked the girls.

"Yeah, that sounds like a good idea," Rhonda Sue replied.

Stevie was still smiling at James. "I know what you're thinking," James said.

"I think you've got a problem on your hands, Hoss."

"Yeah, well, I've got to deal with this."

"You don't deal with problems...you eliminate them."

With that, Stevie jammed some peanuts in this mouth and walked away.

Jerry and Lenny sat down after dancing a few numbers with their dates. Jerry patted James on his back. They knew.

After a few moments, the girls came back to the tables. They made some small talk as the band continued to play some great rock music.

The band returned to the stage after a brief break. They started what would be a string of slow songs.

Catherine quickly came over and grabbed James' arm. "Let's go, Tiger. They're playing our song."

James was completely caught off guard. "Whoa, whoa, take it easy."

"What are you talking about it? Let's go! Let's dance!"

"Catherine, I'm not dancing with you right now."

"You're serious? You'd rather dance with that boring hick?" she said, pointing to Mary.

Rhonda Sue quickly stood up. "Hey, bitch…"

James then jumped in. "She's not a hick. She's my girlfriend. I love her. I don't think I've given you the wrong impression, but if I did, I'm sorry. I don't feel that way about you. You and I are just friends."

"Guess again! We're not even that now!" Catherine then stormed away.

James regained his composure. He stuck his hand out. "Would you like to dance, Mary?"

Mary took his hand and they headed to the dance floor. This time, Mary held him close. "Thank you," she said.

"I guess I owe you a big apology," James replied. "I didn't realize..."

"No. I'm sorry. I shouldn't have been ignoring you. I was just so jealous."

"You were...weren't you?"

"Yeah. I never thought I could be that jealous, but I was. I thought you liked her as more than just friends."

"You want to talk about jealous? When I was at Shooter's party – I think that was the worst feeling I ever had. I heard you were slow dancing with some guy."

"Slow dancing? Oh, that was my cousin, Ray. We danced a couple times."

"Your cousin? Oh, man, do I feel like an idiot."

"He wanted to meet you, but you left so soon."

"Yeah, I know. You kind of gave me the cold shoulder."

"I'm sorry. I was really trying to make you jealous. I didn't even know about the party until Rhonda Sue called me."

James smiled and looked up at the ceiling. "You know what? I have an idea. Why don't we start over?"

"I'm all for that."

They kissed and hugged tightly.

"You hear that?" James asked.

"Earth Angel!" The band started playing one of Mary's favorite songs.

"You are my angel, Mary." James started singing. "I'm just a fool...a fool in love with you..."

"Oh, God. Why don't we just shut up and enjoy our dance," Mary said, laughing.

CHAPTER 45

As great as the rest of the homecoming dance was, James and Mary couldn't wait to be alone that night.

They drove up to Peak's Pointe. It was just on the outskirts of town, on the south side. It was a beautiful autumn evening. There was a chill, but it was not terribly cold. Most of the leaves had fallen from the trees. You could see a barrage of orange lights – signifying the Halloween season.

James and Mary sat in the front seat of his car. At first they said nothing. They just gazed at the lights.

"Thank you for sticking up for me tonight. It really means a lot to me."

"I guess I've been blind," James said. "My friends were telling me about Catherine, but I didn't see it. I've always gotten along with her. I mean – she's always been flirty. But, I never believed all the things everyone said about her."

"Believe them!"

"Really?"

"Well, I know for a fact that she has a history with some of the guys at Crestfield. That's why I got so jealous." She cuddled up even closer to James. "No one's going to cut into my territory."

"Whoa. Keep talking dirty! I like it!"

"You're just lucky you didn't do anything with her. I would have cut your balls off!"

"Geez. Where's this coming from? You never used to talk like that. What happened to my innocent, little Mary?"

"Hmmmm. If I find her, I'll let you know," Mary said, as she titled her head back and puckered her lips.

"Cute," James said, as he playfully put Mary in a headlock.

Mary fixed her hair and looked at James. She stared into his eyes. "Do you want to go in back?" she asked.

"Are you sure?"

"I'm sure."

"It's cramped in back, though."

"I don't mind…if you don't mind."

James and Mary went into the back seat. They kissed for a while. Then they took off each other's clothes, slowly.

It might have been cramped, but it didn't seem to bother them. Their first time, the night of July 4th , would always be very special. But this time it was much slower, and in many ways, even more intimate. For the moment, they completely forgot what they had been fighting about.

CHAPTER 46

"Wow, that's something, Mom," Jennifer said. "I can't picture you with a lot of make- up and high heels."

"Oh, you'd be surprised with some of the things I did. I wasn't as innocent as you may have thought."

"Obviously! Well, at least you were never arrested."

Mary looked straight at Jennifer, and then smiled.

"What? Don't tell me you have a police record - I'll never be the same."

"No, I was never arrested, but we got close," Mary said, with a sparkle in her eye.

"Well, you have to tell me now!"

Mary turned her head and looked up. She cleared her throat. "I think it was the spring before we graduated. It was a Friday night. These jerks had been hanging around Harley's. They were a group of local thugs. They considered themselves a gang. I think a couple of them were high school dropouts. They thought they were so cool."

Jennifer smiled. It made her laugh when her mom used slang from when she was a kid.

"Anyways, their gang leader challenged Stevie to a drag race. Of course, Stevie couldn't turn down the challenge. The boys worked on Stevie's car all week, getting it ready for the race. Well, Stevie decides James is going to ride shotgun with him in the race."

"Where was the race?"

"If I recall, it was on East 12ᵗʰ street. Twelfth street was a very long street that connected the East and West sides of the city."

"I think I know where this is going."

"Yeah, the cops showed up. By that time the race had begun. I was in James' car, and decided to go after them, to see if I could pick him up and get out of there."

"What happened?"

"I did catch up to them. James jumped in the car and we tried to take off."

"Are you serious?"

"Dead serious. One of the cops caught up to us. I don't think we got more than three or four blocks away."

"How much trouble did you get in?"

"We didn't. And you wouldn't believe why."

"Tell me."

"Well, the police officer came up to my window. He wanted to see my license. He then put his flashlight on James. The officer asked me if I was okay. I told him I was." Mary laughed and turned her head from side to side. "I still remember this. James had his West Cannon lettermen's jacket on. The cop starts asking James questions. As it turned out, the officer's son played football for West Cannon several years earlier. So, he told us he never wanted to see us at a drag race again, and let us go."

"All because James played for West Cannon."

"Yep, membership had its privileges."

"What happened to Stevie?"

"He wasn't so lucky. I believe he ended up getting a ticket from the police officer that pulled him over."

"Too bad Stevie didn't play football for West Cannon."

"Yeah, his loss. And you know what the ironic thing was? I recall that before the race Stevie kept telling James to get rid of his jacket. You know, if something happened, it was obvious that James was in high school, attending West Cannon. But James refused to take it off. Had James not had that jacket on, well..."

"You guys were lucky."

"We sure were."

"Well, this totally changes my opinion of you, Mom," Jennifer said.

"Oh, honey, we did so many things together. We sure had a lot of fun. With James, it felt like anything was possible."

Mary went silent for a moment. She closed her eyes.

Jennifer was glad her mom was opening up about her past. It seemed to help her. She also wondered why she rarely had spoken about Jennifer's and Jacqui's father like that. There was something different about Mary when she talked about James. There was a glow – as if a part of her came alive. Jennifer couldn't resist the fact that there was something very uncomfortable about that.

"Honey, I hope you don't mind that I told you about James, and the night of the Homecoming. I hope it's not...what do you kids call it today ...too much information."

Jennifer laughed. "I'm glad you told me. You know you can tell me anything."

"It's not that Jacqui and I don't talk. We do. But, I could always talk to you about personal things."

"You must have really been in love, Mom."

"I was. We were. Those few weeks before Homecoming just ate at me. The thought of James with that Catherine made me crazy."

"Whatever happened to her? Do you know?"

"I heard she was divorced a couple times. It could be more than that."

"Did she ever bother you or Mr. Evans again?"

"Not that I remember. James really put her in her place that night. But James being the person that he was – I had heard he wrote her an apology letter, and he still considered her a friend. I didn't say anything. I figured he was my boyfriend – not hers –and that's all that really mattered."

"Mom, what do you think happened to him? I mean, from everything you've said, and from his letters, he seemed like a mature kid. He seemed like he had his life figured out."

"I know, dear. I've been wondering the same thing. I wonder if because he had his life figured out, it scared him when he found out I was pregnant. Maybe he thought his life was over."

"I'm sure he was scared, but why didn't he try to keep in touch with you? Why did he leave you when you needed him most?"

"I wish I knew. I wish I knew. We were both so young."

"Did he ever tell you what happened to him?"

"What do you mean?"

"Do you know if he went to college? Did he end up getting a good job? Did he move out of town?"

"Hmmm. You know, dear, I don't think he ever said. I don't think we even talked about that."

"What are your plans? Are you still going to talk to him?"

"Well, it's pretty difficult not to say something. We see each other just about every day."

"Aren't you curious with what happened to him?"

"I guess so. I wasn't at first. I was too upset. But it seems to feel better talking about it."

Mary paused, and looked out the window. She took a deep breath. "I just hope I didn't hurt your brother too much."

"He'll be okay, Mom. You're going to have to give him time."

"Well, I know he can be very stubborn. When he believes in something, or commits to something, he usually doesn't waiver."

Jennifer got up and gave Mary a hug. Tears started flowing down Mary's face. "We'll get through this, Mom. We have a strong family, and we'll get through this."

Mary wanted to be optimistic, but she was more of a realist than Jennifer. Her instincts told her there were many rocky days ahead. Her wisdom told her there was no way things would ever be the same – especially between Anthony and her.

CHAPTER 47

"Good morning, Mary."

"Good morning, Ben."

"How are you doing this morning?" he asked as he served scrambled eggs and toast to Mary.

"Oh, okay, I guess. Where is everybody?"

Ben gave a quick look. "Yeah, I see what you mean. Maybe everyone slept in today, "he said sarcastically.

Mary let out a laugh. "You know most of us don't sleep well at night."

"That's because you guys sleep through most of the day," Ben shot back.

"Hey now, just serve breakfast, young man."

Ben was one of Mary's favorites. She never saw him in a bad mood. He kept things light, and brought some much-needed spark to a sometimes dull cafeteria.

"Wait a minute...what's today?"

"It's Friday, Ben."

"Ah...I bet a lot of people went on that bus trip to Pleasant View Mall."

"Oh, that's right."

"You didn't want to go, Mary?"

"No. I asked my daughters if they were interested but they couldn't make it."

"Well, it looks like a lot of leftovers for you, Mary."

Mary put her hands over her stomach. "Oh, this is quite enough for me."

"Looks like you are all alone this morning – it appears everyone at your table must be on that bus trip."

"It'll be a very quiet breakfast. Do you know if any of the men went on the bus trip?"

"Let me check, Mary." Ben opened the door to the kitchen and stuck his head inside. "Hey, Paul, do you know if any of the gentlemen went on the trip?"

Mary laughed. "Heck I could have done that."

Ben came back out. "Looks like Stan, David and Ron must have gone – we don't have meals for them."

Mary was curious about James. She had not seen him in a few days. "I guess Mr. Evans went to?"

"Mr. Evans?" Ben asked, quite surprised. "He's not here anymore," he said matter-of-factly.

Mary didn't comprehend. "He's not here today?"

"Today, tomorrow, the next day," Ben replied. "He left earlier in the week."

"Where did he go? Is he in the hospital?"

"No, he's not in the hospital. He's no longer at Rosemont."

Mary felt completely stunned. What did he mean he just left? Was he running again?

CHAPTER 48

"Hey, Mom."

"Hi, Jacqui," Mary said in a low voice.

"You okay? Not feeling well?"

"I'm okay."

Jacqui bent down and got close up to Mary's face. "Something's wrong. Tell me."

"Did you know that Mr. Evans left?"

"He left? Where did he go?"

"I don't know. I just heard that he left Rosemont."

"I can't believe that. He bailed on you again!"

"Oh, honey, I don't think he bailed." Mary was trying to put a positive spin on things.

"How can you say that?"

"I mean….he doesn't have any obligations to me. What happened…happened a long time ago."

Jacqui was exasperated. "It might have happened a long time ago…but it seems to me that it's happening again."

"Well…" Mary paused.

"Seriously, Mom. He just found out that he's Anthony's father – and he leaves? That's horrible."

"I just wished I knew where he went. I'd still like to talk to him."

"I'd like to talk to him!" Jacqui snapped back.

"Please don't do anything."

"What do you think I'm going to do?"

"I know you, Jacqui. When you get something in your head, you can't let it go. Please tell me you won't jump off the handle."

"There you go, with your old sayings again," Jacqui mused. "Alright, I'll let you handle it, but I want to be kept updated."

"Fair enough." Mary figured she had Jacqui calmed down – for now.

CHAPTER 49

"Mr. Evans, there's someone here to see you," Sandra Huff said in a deep voice. Sandra was an aide at SunnyHill Assisted Living. To the residents of SunnyHill, it was anything but "sunny." Apparently, their employees felt the same way.

"A visitor?"

"Yes, a visitor. You know – someone who comes and visits..."

"I know what a visitor is, thank you." In the very short time James was at SunnyHill he learned that residents needed to stand up to the staff. You couldn't take shit from them, he learned. Stand up to the bully, so to speak.

After coming down from her "high horse", Sandra assisted James to the front entrance. He couldn't believe it. He stood there, speechless. "How did you know I was here?"

"Hello. I didn't mean to startle you." Anthony had snow in his hair and it was falling off his long coat.

Anthony held out his hand. They shook.

"Oh, Sandra, this is my...this is Anthony."

"Nice to meet you, sir," she said in her low voice.

"Nice to meet you, ma'am."

"Um....did you want to sit somewhere?" James asked.

"Why don't the two of you sit in the cafeteria," Sandra butted in.

The cafeteria was dark. It had already been cleaned up after dinner. They sat at a small round table. They thought Sandra had left, but she came back with two cups of coffee.

"For me, too?" James asked.

"Yes, I got one for you too. Don't let it get to your head. It won't happen again."

With that, Sandra left them alone, along with a pot of coffee.

"She seems like a handful," Anthony said.

"Ah, she's nothing but a bully. She thinks her shit doesn't stink."

"Are they all like that here?"

'Not all of them, I guess. But there is definitely a certain attitude here. They don't go out of their way here."

"You don't get that warm, fuzzy feeling here?"

"No, not here. But back to my original question. How did you know I was here?"

"Well, if I said a little birdie told me, would you believe me?"

James laughed slightly to himself.

"Actually, the person at Rosemont's front desk kind of let it out."

"Christ. It figures. She could never keep a secret. Isn't there a law now about privacy?"

"Don't be mad at her. I was actually trying my best to get it from her. I can be pretty persuasive."

"I suppose your mom knows I'm here?"

"No, I didn't say a word. They found out you left Rosemont. My sister told me. I figured you would let her know if you wanted."

"Thanks, I appreciate that."

They both paused as if looking for the next thing to say.

"How long are you in town?"

"For a few more days."

"I have to be honest. I didn't expect to see you."

"Well, I have to be honest. I didn't expect you to leave Rosemont."

"Is your family upset?"

"I know my sister, Jacqui, is."

"I'm sorry for that – I really am."

"Why did you leave? I always heard it was difficult to find an assisted living facility."

"You can call it what it is – a nursing home. And I guess I thought I brought shame to your family, and to myself. I thought it would be best if I stayed out of your lives. Certainly, I thought it would be best if Mary didn't have to run into me every day."

James took a long sip of coffee. Anthony let him continue talking.

'I don't know. Maybe I am running away again."

"How did you find out about this place?"

A guy moved into Rosemont. He was assigned to my table. He said he was at SunnyHill. I guess he had been trying to get into Rosemont."

"So you ended up taking his spot at SunnyHill."

"Yeah, he gave me a contact, and I quickly called SunnyHill. They gave me his old room."

"So, how do you like it here?"

"Do you want me to lie, or do you want the other version?"

Anthony got a chuckle out of that. "So I take it's not what you expected?"

"Don't tell this to the people at Rosemont, but Rosemont is heaven compared to this place."

"I'm sorry to hear that."

"This place just isn't as clean. The halls smell awful. I think some of the people shit themselves and no one jumps to do anything about it. Ah, hell, nothing I can do about it now."

James continued.

"I don't want to be too forward, but why did you try to find me here? I figured I would be the last person you wanted to see."

"I'm not going to lie. I was not just upset with you, but with my mom as well."

"I know. I wish I could change things."

Anthony looked into his cup. "Do you want a refill?"

"Sure, thanks."

Anthony got up and grabbed another pot of coffee. Sandra had left a second pot.

Anthony sat back down. "I have to ask you something. Something I've been wondering about."

James took a drink of his coffee, and nodded.

"Did you ever try to find my mother? Did you ever wonder what happened to her?

James gave a little smile as he looked down at his cup. "I thought about her more than you could imagine. From time to time things would remind me of her."

"Like what things – can I ask?"

"Well, some of the hardest times were after high school. I eventually joined the Army. I remember a lot of the guys receiving letters and pictures from their wives, or girlfriends. That hurt. I had absolutely nothing to look forward to."

"I don't want to sound mean, but really, didn't you put yourself in that position?"

"Yeah, I guess I did. I have to be honest. When Mary first told me she was pregnant, I wasn't exactly what you would call a pillar of strength."

James thought back to that time...

CHAPTER 50

GRADUATION WEEK

TUESDAY

"Hey."

Mary jumped. "Oh, you scared me. I didn't expect to see you."

"Sorry." James was sitting on Mary's front porch. They had put out their glider and other furniture for the summer. It was 7:45 a.m. "Can I drive you to school?"

"Um, sure."

Mary was quiet on the way to school.

"You okay?"

"Uh, yeah," she said.

James could tell she was pre-occupied. She continued looking out her window.

"Well, here you go. Have a good day."

Mary just realized they were already at Crestfield. "Thanks," she said, opening her door.

"Hey, are you forgetting something?"

Mary gave a quick smile. She gave James a kiss on the cheek.

James didn't give it too much of a second thought and headed to school.

The following night James called Mary. "Hey, how's it going?"

"Ok."

"Wow. You sound depressed. Did you forget this is the last week of high school?"

"I know. I'm just tired, I guess. Finals have been hard so far."

"Finals? Don't tell me you're worried about finals. Next week, it won't even matter."

Mary paused. "I just want to finish up."

"Okay, okay, I understand…I guess. I'll call you tomorrow, alright?"

"Okay."

CHAPTER 51

Later that evening Mary called James.

"Hey, I thought you'd be studying. You took my advice, huh?"

"We have to talk, Jimmy."

"What's wrong? You sound so serious lately."

"We really need to talk."

"Ok. Do you want to meet somewhere?"

"If we could, I'd like to...hold on a minute."

James could hear Mary yelling something in the background. She got back on the phone. She tried talking again but James could hear her mother.

"I'm going to have to call you back." Mary sounded frustrated...and very upset.

With that, she hung up.

James wondered what she wanted to talk about. But he had big news for her!

CHAPTER 52

FRIDAY – LAST DAY OF HIGH SCHOOL

At West Cannon, you could see the distinction between the boys and girls. It couldn't be any clearer. The guys were slapping "high fives" with each other. They'd been waiting for this for four years! Some would go on to college, but for many this would be their last day of formal education.

To the contrary, many of the girls shed tears and hugged. They wrote in each other's yearbooks. They wrote that they would stay in touch, and would remain friends forever. But, how realistic was that? Deep down, some knew that they might never see some of their classmates again.

James completed his Physics exam, and that was it. He met up with Stevie, Lenny and Jerry. James rode shotgun in Stevie's car. It occurred to him that high school was not the only thing ending. Would he, Stevie, Lenny and Jerry remain best friends? To their surprise, Lenny had recently announced that he was joining the Marines in mid-July. Stevie and Jerry had no immediate plans. Stevie had been working part time at Harry's Auto Service. He knew his shit about cars, and it was assumed he would continue working there. Jerry helped on weekends at his dad's tavern. He cleaned and washed dishes. Perhaps someday he would take over for his dad.

For James, the sky was the limit. He was going to college and was going to play football. He chose Ohio University. He would study Architecture and Engineering, while getting an opportunity to play college football.

None of the boys said much as Stevie took each of them home. *Maybe he didn't give them enough credit*, James thought. *Maybe they were feeling the same way.*

CHAPTER 53

If there was a feeling of melancholy earlier, it was long gone that evening. Many of the popular seniors would be meeting at the Peninsula. There was reason to celebrate.

They started gathering at Beach 8. James met the guys there at 7:30. Mary told him she would meet him there later.

Some of the guys were playing football on the sand. Several of the kids were playing volleyball. Those who were brave tested the water. It might have been June, but the lake was still pretty cold.

As the sun set and the air got cooler, they built a bon fire. It wasn't long before it worked off the chill.

Mary and the Hearts showed up. James went over and hugged Mary. "Hey, girls." "Can we go for a walk – I have some big news to tell you," James said to Mary.

"Sure, I wanted to talk to you anyway."

They walked along the beach water. The tide was coming in. The waves were slamming against the shore. They held hands as they got further away from the others.

"How were your finals?"

"I did okay. I'm glad they're over," Mary said. "How did you do?"

James chuckled. "I didn't study a lick. I didn't care at this point. I'm in!"

Mary stopped and looked at James. "You picked a college?"

"Yep. That's what I wanted to talk to you about. Drum roll, please. It's Ohio University. I'm going to Ohio University."

Mary didn't say anything at first.

"Wow, that's great news, Jimmy," James said sarcastically.

"I'm sorry. That is great news. I'm very proud of you," Mary said, somewhat sheepishly.

"Can you believe it? I couldn't wait to tell you. I wanted to wait for the perfect moment."

"Wow, you're moving away?"

"Yeah, but it's not too far. A lot closer than Illinois."

"Yeah, that's true."

"Geez. I have to be honest, Mary. I thought you'd be more excited."

"I am. I guess I'm just thinking about you leaving – especially at a time like this."

"What do you mean?'

"Nothing.....nothing."

"Hey, it's going to be alright. Like I said, I'll still be pretty close. I can come home on breaks and some weekends. Heck, you can come up and see me. You'd have to tell your dad you're visiting one of your girlfriends," James said, laughing.

Mary wasn't laughing. She knew there was the possibility of James going away to college. But, there had been issues with how much scholarship money he would receive. He and his mom didn't have money to pay for college, and they would need a lot of assistance. By this time, she figured James would be staying in town. As she thought about it, she knew this was a big moment for James. She had to put on her best face.

"I am really proud of you." She gave him a big hug.

"Hey, we'll make this work. You'll see- it's no big deal."

They started walking back. "I can't believe I'm going to be playing college football."

It was the happiest she had seen him in a while. This was his dream. He was going to college, and he was going to play football. Plus, it was the last day of high school. Why wouldn't he be excited?

The bigger question now was – how could she tell him her news?

CHAPTER 54

Crestfield's graduation was the following day. Their school wasn't very big, so students and family members were able to fit in the auditorium.

It was a typical ceremony. It was festive, but wouldn't have the pomp and circumstance of West Cannon's graduation on Sunday.

James sat toward the back. He saw Mary's parents up front, so he wasn't too close to them.

It was a nice ceremony. Some of the kids were excited. Some of the girls were crying. James noticed that Mary seemed neither happy nor sad. What was bothering her? Was she simply upset that James was leaving? James had noticed that she had been acting differently, well before he told her about Ohio University. Was there something else?

After the ceremony, a reception was held in the cafeteria. James waited until after Mary talked to her friends. She saw him and walked over to him.

"Hi."

"Hey. Congratulations. I didn't want to bother you. I know you wanted to talk to your friends."

'Yeah, I think it's starting to hit us that we are going our separate ways."

James gave her an expression as if he understood. He gave her a hug. Mary seemed to have tears in her eyes, but she was able to hold them in.

At that point Mary's grandparents from her dad's side, walked over.

"Congratulations honey. We're so proud of you," her grandmother said.

Her grandfather then gave her a big hug. He had some expensive camera equipment hanging from his neck. He quickly took a few photos of Mary and her grandmother. He then gave Mary a big squeeze.

"This is my boyfriend, Jimmy," Mary told them.

"Well hello, Jimmy. It's nice to meet you," her grandmother said.

"That's my Nana, and this is Papa," Mary said, proudly.

Her Papa shook James' hand. It was a very firm handshake. "Nice to meet you, Jimmy."

"It's nice to meet you both."

Wow. These were Mary's father's parents? At least from first impressions they seemed like really nice people. Was Mary's father adopted, James wondered. He laughed to himself.

"I'm sorry we had not met you before," Nana said. "We live in Florida. We like to travel a lot. We're enjoying our retirement years."

"That's nice. Florida? Wow, that's quite a trip."

Papa interjected. "It is. But we like to stop along the way and see some different things."

Mary's parents came over. Her mom was gracious and seemed genuinely pleased that James came to Mary's graduation. Her father said little. Nothing new there.

Mary's parents held a small party at their house later that day. James finally had a chance to meet some of Mary's closest relatives.

James and Mary went outside to the backyard. They sat on a swing that had a canopy over it.

"Your relatives seem like really nice people," James said.

"Thanks. Yeah, they're really down to earth."

She took hold of James' hand. "You really seemed to have made a good impression. In fact, I think a couple of my cousins like you."

"Oh yeah? Which ones?"

"Well, my cousin Katherine thinks you're cute."

James let out a loud laugh.

"What's so funny?"

"Katherine, huh? Isn't it ironic that "Katherine" likes me?" James smiled.

"Oh, please, that's not even funny. My cousin's nothing like the "Catherine" you're thinking of. It's not even spelled the same..."

"Oh, it's not even spelled the same now, isn't it..." James said, as he playfully poked Mary in the side.

It was the first time he'd seen Mary smile in quite a long time.

"Thanks for coming tonight."

James said nothing.

"Hey, are you there?"

"Huh? Oh, sorry. I was listening to the sirens. I was saying my prayer."

"You were what? Praying?"

"Yeah. Did you hear those sirens?"

"Yeah."

"Sounded like a fire truck or ambulance. Not sure. I think it was an ambulance."

"So?"

"Well, whenever I hear a siren, I say a quick prayer --- usually a Hail Mary. I figure someone might be hurt, or sick...or worse. Maybe they could use a prayer."

Mary thought for a minute that this might be a good time to tell him, but she didn't want to ruin this moment. She figured maybe she could use some of those Hail Marys.

CHAPTER 55

Graduation day at West Cannon was a big event. Because of the number of students and family members, the ceremony was held in the football stadium. It hadn't rained on graduation day for several years. Their luck continued. It looked like a beautiful day.

The mood was light. The students were downright giddy. There was much more of a party atmosphere than at Crestfield's ceremony.

As the students entered the stadium, they sat on wooden chairs, facing the north end zone. They listened to the student government president, Lance Wilkerson, talk about making a difference in society. That was followed up with speeches by the Principal and the School District Superintendent, who basically said the same thing.

James looked around the stadium. *A lot of great moments here*, he thought. He was sitting not far from the spot where he made the game saving interception against Rottstown. What a feeling that was! He looked up at the locker room, where the team would come out before every game. Unless you played the game there was no way to describe the rush – that feeling that came over you as you walked through the throng of students on each side. They would cheer and slap you on your shoulder pads or helmet. There were many memories, but most of all he started to realize he'd miss most of the friendships he made with the guys on the team. They would be going their separate ways. Would they get together at reunions and talk about the "good old days?"

James continued to look around. He eventually found Mary on the side, not too far from the top. She seemed to be listening intently to the speakers.

As the students were called to the stage, the Principal would state whether each student had been accepted to a college. It wasn't a great percentage. Some didn't have the money or motivation to go to college. Many would be able to find jobs after high school. A lot of them were interested in paychecks. James felt very fortunate.

After the ceremony, James went through the crowd, hugging a lot of the girls and wishing them well in their futures. He shook hands with many of the guys. It was a chaotic scene as family members flooded the field. James found his mom and gave her a hug.

"Congratulations, kid."

"Thanks, Mom."

'I'm proud of you. You really did it. I could say you're a young man now, but I guess you've been a young man for quite some time now."

There was sadness in her eyes. James knew what she meant. She wasn't able to attend his games. As a single mother, she worked so much to make sure she could pay the mortgage. James often felt cheated. He didn't have a father, and his mother often was not home. But as he stood there with his mom, it occurred to him that a lot of the things he had been able to accomplish were due to the sacrifices his mother made. "Thanks for everything," he told his mom.

His mother smiled and gave him a big hug. She was never more proud than at that moment. "Going to a party?"

"Yeah, Ralphy's having a party at his house." Ralph Jones was heading to an Ivy League college. He was very smart - and his family was very rich. His dad owned a number of clothing stores in the tri-state area. Their house was huge.

"Just be careful - and not too late."

"Okay. No problem."

James spotted Mary at one of the end zones. He walked up to her and gave her a hug. "You just missed my mom."

"No I didn't."

"You saw her?"

"We talked before the ceremony. Actually we talked for quite a while."

"Nothing bad, I hope."

"Why? Do you have a guilty conscience?"

"No, just wondering…"

"She's really proud of you – I can tell you that."

"What about you?"

"You know I'm very proud of you."

"Show me," James said, as he pointed to his cheek.

Mary gave him a kiss. "We really need to talk, Jimmy."

"About what?"

"We need to talk – but away from here."

A group of guys came over to where James and Mary were standing. "Evans, let's go party," one of them said. Somebody else then jumped on James' back.

"Later guys, give me a minute."

"No, go ahead," Mary said, sounding frustrated.

"Are you sure? Can I pick you up later? Do you want to go to Ralphy's party with me?"

"Yeah, I'll go."

With that, James took off. Mary knew this was going to be extremely difficult.

CHAPTER 56

Ralphy wasn't an obnoxious person. But, he didn't mind showing off his house.

His parents were at the ceremony that afternoon, but as soon as it was over, they were on their way to Orlando, Florida. His father was thinking about expanding his business, well beyond their local region. He usually traveled for business, often taking Ralphy's mother with him. Ralphy certainly didn't mind. He told them he was having a few friends over, but even Ralphy had no idea how word had spread, and how many people would be coming to his house.

The party would be similar to others they had attended during their senior year – with one exception. This time, they wouldn't see each other the following Monday. For James this would also be a party like no other.

James and Mary arrived a little later. James had already been feeling pretty good. He had been out with a few of guys that afternoon. Mary had not said much on the way to Ralphy's house.

"You really need to loosen up, "Mar". School's out, man!"

Mary wasn't in the mood to party. James couldn't understand it, and quite frankly he was getting frustrated with the way she had been acting. He told her so.

"Come here," James said, as he took her arm and led her to the side of the house. "I'm not sure what the problem is, but I am really getting annoyed with your attitude. I'm sorry – I don't want to sound mean, but what the hell is your problem?"

"I'm pregnant."

James' face instantly turned red. "What?"

Mary took a deep breath. "I'm pregnant." She couldn't hold it in any longer.

"Are you sure? Maybe something's wrong...maybe..."

"I'm sure, Jimmy."

"This can't be..."

"Jimmy, I took a blood test – it's positive."

James turned his back and walked away from Mary. He put his arms over his head. He then turned around. "How can this be? We were careful."

"I know. I know. But it happened."

James gave Mary a cold stare. "You sound like you wanted this to happen."

"Excuse me?"

"This shouldn't have happened. I think you wanted this to happen."

"Are you fucking crazy?"

James knew that Mary was really mad now. He had only heard Mary use that word one other time - and that had to do with Catherine. But, he couldn't let it go.

"It all adds up. You've been so down about me leaving. Was this a way to try to keep me here?"

Mary was beside herself. "This is utter nonsense. That might be the dumbest thing you ever said. I've never wanted anything but the best for you. I would never do that to you. I can't even believe you would think that."

James thought this time before he spoke. "You're right. I'm sorry. I don't know what I'm saying. I just...I just can't believe it. I had my whole life in front of me. Everything was falling into place."

"We had our whole lives ahead of us," Mary reminded James.

"That's what I meant."

"Did you?"

"I'm just saying --- man, I have a chance to go to college and play football. How many guys can say that?"

"What are you saying?"

"I don't know. I just can't believe this is happening."

"Well, this isn't about you anymore. It's not even about you and me. It's about the three of us. It's about our baby."

CHAPTER 57

PRESENT DAY

Anthony sat back in his chair. For the first time, he tried putting himself in James' shoes. How would Anthony have acted at that age if he found out he was going to be a father?

"Wow, I guess the news that my mom was pregnant had to be overwhelming."

"It was for all of us. I mean, this wasn't supposed to happen to us. This stuff happened to other people, you know. I should have had so much more faith in Mary – in us. Looking back, there was no way she would have given up her baby. "

"If her father had told you the truth – that she was keeping her baby – would that have changed your mind?"

James was floored. The question was direct, and it was being asked by his son. "That is a very good question. I don't know if I would have done anything differently no matter what happened. I guess...I guess at that moment I was so wrapped up with my own concerns for college, and football...I just don't know how to answer that."

James was worried how Anthony would react. But, Anthony showed very little reaction. Actually, Anthony very much appreciated his honesty. He thought maybe he'd come here, and listen to his father talk about how he was now going to try to make up for all the wrong he had done. But, to Anthony's surprise they were having a very open and straightforward conversation. Anthony felt much better about that.

What Anthony didn't realize was that James was just as anxious to find out about him.

"So, where did you go to college?"

"I went to Penn State."

"Wow, that's great. You got a great education, then."

"Yeah, I enjoyed it. I made a lot of new friends. I learned so much."

"You studied business?"

"Mmmhmm. Finance."

"How did you end up in Boston?"

"When I was a senior there was a large job fair held at the school. There were employers from all over the country. They were conducting preliminary interviews. Just basic stuff. I interviewed with a few companies. One of them was Wardner-Haines Financial. Their main office was in Boston. I eventually went up there for a more formal interview. They ended up offering me a job."

"Things worked out."

"They sure did. I was lucky. I actually had a job waiting for me at graduation."

James faced turned to a smile. "I always wondered what Fenway Park looked like up close."

"It's magical. It really is. It's a great city, actually. I mean the harbor, Bunker Hill, Paul Revere......there's just so much history."

"You like that stuff, huh?"

"Oh, yeah. I think I had told you that I follow baseball and other sports, but I'm not obsessed with it. I have a lot of interests.

One of them is learning more and more about our nation's history. It intrigues me."

James had to feel good, even if it was only he that knew it. Anthony seemed to have a sense of curiosity, and a quest for knowledge. James had that when he was younger. At the same time, he could tell Anthony was principled, and very purpose-driven. James also had those qualities when he was young – he just didn't maintain those qualities.

"So you met Lori there?"

"Yes. She's actually from Rhode Island. But she studied in Boston, and got a job there."

"What does she do?"

"She works with disadvantaged kids."

"Wow. Good for her. She likes to have an effect on people."

"Yes. Yes. She does. She has a lot more patience than I do." Anthony thought about his wife at that moment. "We have a daughter, Kristy. She's in school. Good kid. She studies real hard."

It hit James that he was a grandfather. Maybe not a grandfather in the traditional sense. But, nonetheless, biologically he was still a grandfather. He would love to meet his granddaughter.

When Anthony left that night, he felt a calm that he had not felt since bringing Mary to Rosemont. For the first time, he saw a more human side of James. He didn't just want to hear about him from his mother. He needed to sit with him – to look into his eyes. He wanted to see what was in his soul. He saw James as a man who seemed to have a lot of regrets. Not just about Anthony, but life in general. Anthony was still very hurt. It would take a long time for that to ease. But, he also felt empathy for James.

CHAPTER 58

"How are you?"

Mary was reclining in her chair, with a book opened on her lap. She had fallen asleep.

"Sorry – didn't know you were asleep," Anthony said.

"That's okay. I just dozed off. I do that a lot."

"Good book?"

Mary picked up the book and looked at the front cover. "Pretty good. It's a collection of stories. Stories about everyday miracles."

Anthony made a grin.

"I know. I know. You don't believe in miracles."

"I'm just more of a realist. I believe in what I can see."

"Ah, where did I go wrong?"

They both laughed.

"So, you heading back home?"

"Yeah, I said good bye to Jacqui and Jennifer. I just have to get gassed up before I hit the highway."

"Just be careful. Don't try to push it. Find a hotel if you start feeling tired."

"I'll be okay. I usually stop a few times, and grab a cup of coffee – lots of sugar."

"Well, I appreciate you coming by. I'm glad you got to come home for a few days."

"Yeah, it was a good visit. I'm glad I came in."

Deep down, Anthony wanted to tell Mary he knew where James was. But his instincts told him to keep that to himself...at least for now. He gave Mary a hug. He then said goodbye to the employees at the nurses' desk.

As he walked out, he saw Jane Benson –Nurse Benson as she was known.

"Bundle up. It's cold out there," she told Anthony.

"Yeah, they said the temperature was going to drop. "

"You're Mr. Evans' son, aren't you?"

"Yes." It sounded strange for Anthony to say that.

"Please tell your dad that Nurse Benson said "hi". "I miss seeing him."

"I'll do that."

Before Anthony could get through the doors, Jane kept talking.

"I hope he's okay. I feel so badly for him."

Anthony stopped and turned towards Jane. She continued. "My grandfather had kidney problems. It seemed like he was always on dialysis. He really suffered. Well, I'm praying for your dad. I pray they find him a donor."

Anthony walked slowly through the doors. He stopped and wondered if he had heard correctly. Did James need a donor? He needed a new kidney? Suddenly it felt very cold outside.

CHAPTER 59

Anthony headed out on Interstate 90 for the long ride back to Boston. The news about James startled him. Was he dying, and if so, how much time did the doctors give him?

He drove on, cutting through New York State. The weather wasn't bad. It was cold, but it wasn't snowing. Weather wise he picked a good day to drive back.

What was James' plan? Did he intend on telling him, or telling Mary? If not, Anthony saw that as selfish. After what they've all been through, how could he keep that a secret? He was disturbed by that thought.

Anthony was starting to get tired. He'd been so focused with the news about James that he didn't realize he was running dangerously low on gas. He stopped at the next service area.

It felt good to stretch. After using the restroom, he walked around the bend to the food court. He couldn't tell if people were lined up for Burger King or the Chinese takeout next to it. The lines seemed to merge.

"Geez."

"My sentiments exactly."

Anthony turned around. He smiled to the gentleman behind him. "I didn't think it would be this busy," he said to the stranger.

"That makes two of us. But I have a taste for a bacon double cheeseburger. I'd stand here for hours if I had to."

"Wow. You do have a taste, huh?"

The man laughed. "You probably think I'm crazy."

"No," Anthony replied. Then he quickly changed his tune. "Yes." They laughed. "I'm Anthony, by the way."

"Christopher. Nice to meet you."

"I'm just looking for a large cup of coffee."

"I think you're stuck here. There are no vending machines."

"No machines? Are you sure?"

"Been here plenty of times – no machines. They took them out in 1999."

Anthony thought it odd that he would know that. The stranger sounded credible. And as much as this guy wanted a bacon double cheeseburger, Anthony was dying for a cup of coffee. Like Christopher, he was willing to wait.

It wasn't as bad as they thought. Twelve minutes. Bad enough, but it could have been worse.

Anthony took his coffee outside. He looked up at the bright blue sky.

"Beautiful, isn't it?" Christopher had startled Anthony.

"Yes, it is."

Christopher stared at the sky. "It never gets old to me – looking up into the sky. How's your coffee?"

"Good. Nice and hot. It was worth the wait."

Anthony looked at Christopher. He noticed he was holding a soda.

"You ate your sandwich already? Boy, you were hungry."

"You noticed that, huh?"

Anthony was getting ready to leave when Christopher kept the conversation going. "So, where ya headed?"

"Back home to Boston."

"Ah, Beantown. Great City. Rich tradition. Can't go wrong there."

"Yeah, I like it there. How about you? What's your destination?"

"Headed North."

Anthony thought that was a strange answer but didn't press him on it.

Christopher continued. 'I love traveling – seeing all the great things this world has to offer. Just feels great to be alive," he said, as he turned to Anthony.

"Yeah, I guess."

"You guess? That didn't sound reassuring."

"Well, just dealing with a lot of stuff lately – a lot of family stuff." Anthony was wondering why he was telling a stranger all of this.

"Mmmm-hmmm. That can be tricky. Family issues can get complicated. Sometimes you just have to take a step back , and listen to what your heart says."

"Hmmm. I'm not sure what my heart says. I can't even think straight anymore."

Christopher took a drink of his soda. "Man, that was refreshing. Let me ask you – are you someone that likes to have everything in control – you know, everything in front of you?"

Anthony thought for a moment. "Yeah, I guess you could say that. I know that I like to look forward. I'm getting tired of dealing with old issues – especially when I had no control or say over them."

"Oh. Some old closets opened up?"

"They opened alright. I wish things were exactly like they were months ago. Things were a lot less complicated then."

"You could say that you were in control then?"

Anthony chuckled. "Yeah, that I was."

Christopher paused. He looked back up into the sky. "Did you ever notice though that when we think that we're so in control of everything, we're usually not? Heck, life can be fun sometimes when things are downright messy. Maybe not always fun, but at least interesting."

Anthony took a sip of his coffee, when he noticed it was just about empty.

"Oh, here," Christopher said, as he handed Anthony another cup of coffee.

"I thought you were drinking soda?"

"I am. I just had a feeling we may end up talking more so I also got you another coffee."

"Thank you. Thanks very much." Anthony couldn't figure out how he knew they would end up talking more, but he sure did appreciate the extra cup. On the other hand, it did seem strange that this cup was still very hot. This guy gave Anthony the creeps. But he also seemed kind of polarizing.

"So there's trouble on the home front?"

"What do you do when you're torn between wanting to get to know someone better, yet feeling like you should hate them at the same time?"

"You referring to marriage?"

They looked at each other, and both let out a big laugh. The stranger had a sense of humor.

"I'm just kidding, of course. Marriage is the best institution. I just wanted to see you laugh."

"That was a good one. Well, where do I begin? I find my biological father after many years. He's in a nursing home. I didn't even know he was alive. Now, I find out he's sick, although he didn't tell me that himself. I want to help him, but I want to hate him too. I keep trying to put things into perspective, but I'm not sure I can."

"Sounds like you're trying to control things."

"Well…"

Before Anthony could continue, he realized maybe Christopher was right. He was trying to control things – control how he felt, control how Mary felt, control how James felt.

"You see, sometimes things have to play out in due course. The harder you try to alter that, the more frustrated you'll become."

"How did you get to be so wise?"

"Oh, I've been around. Had some good experiences as a teacher, counselor, mentor. Heck, when I was young, I was a carpenter." Anthony looked at him.

"The point is, life's too short to try to make everything happen your way. Things are going to happen. It's how you respond to it that defines you."

Christopher took a final gulp of his soda. "You say you don't know what your heart is saying? Sure you do. You first have to open up your heart. Maybe it's telling you that you've been provided with a great gift."

"A gift?"

"Mmmm-hmmm. An opportunity. An opportunity to possibly help your father – no matter what others may think, and not because you think you have to. An opportunity to change a life."

"I guess that doesn't come along every day."

'Oh, yes, it does. We just think of it in large, dramatic terms. It doesn't have to be."

"All I know is that ever since he entered the picture, nothing has been the same."

"For you?"

"Yeah, my life's been turned around. " Anthony spoke quickly - then paused.

"Mmmm-hmmmm. I wonder if your dad's life has been turned around."

Anthony seemed a little perturbed. "I'm not saying he hasn't been affected, but he's in a..."

"In a nursing home? Yeah, I suppose you're right. He's older and he's sick...."

"I didn't mean it like that. I just feel like I had my whole life ahead. I can't explain it."

Christopher put his hand on Anthony's shoulder. "I bet your dad felt that way sometimes when he was young."

Christopher turned and looked toward the highway. 'Well, I better get going. Got to go help a friend. It was nice meeting you, young man. Have a safe trip."

"Thank you, sir. I wish you safe travels as well. Thanks for the coffee."

As Christopher started to walk away, he turned around towards Anthony. "You know, your dad's like a lot of other seniors. They just need a little help, a little love. But for some reason we make them feel guilty...like they've messed up our lives. Let me just share something with you. The greatest gift you can give in this life is "sacrifice." Giving of your time, giving of your talents. Helping others. That's really what life is all about."

As Anthony got back on the highway and drove for a while, he thought about his conversation with Christopher. Christopher was right, he realized.

Anthony felt guilty. When he went to visit his mom, he had to admit that he couldn't wait to leave. When he visited, he thought that was enough. He felt like he'd done his duty. He never really looked at it from the perspective of Mary or James. That bothered him.

As he drove past the exits around Albany, he thought about James. How sick was he? And could he help him?

In his side view mirror, he could see a vehicle with bright lights coming up at a very high rate of speed. *What an asshole,* Anthony thought.

As the vehicle approached, it seemed to slow down. Anthony turned to his left. It was Christopher! Christopher glanced over to his right. He gave Anthony a smile. Anthony noticed a few bumper stickers on his car: "God is my co-pilot." Anthony hadn't seen that one in decades. The one next to it read: "My co-pilot knows the way." Christopher had a way with words. But it was the third one that really caught Anthony's eye: "Always Headed North." He thought that was interesting. Then it hit him. At the rest stop Christopher had said he was headed north. Anthony assumed he meant upper New York State, or Canada. But they were headed east towards Massachusetts. There must have been a deeper meaning there.

As he drove another 30 miles or so, traffic came to a sudden stop. He assumed it was either road construction or an accident. It was an accident.

Traffic moved at a snail's pace as he got closer to the accident site. There were two vehicles in the median. Both were damaged pretty badly. One person was sitting up and was being attended by paramedics. As Anthony drove slowly by the site he saw someone being lifted into an ambulance. Suddenly, Anthony stopped. Luckily traffic was only moving at five miles per hour or he would have also been in an accident. He looked closer. It couldn't be! Christopher was giving CPR to one of the victims. How did he end up at the accident scene? At the rest area, he said he had to go help a friend...

CHAPTER 60

"Hello, Jacqui, how are you?" She snuck up on Jacqui.

"Shirley, Hi." Shirley was an old family friend. Jacqui didn't notice her standing next to her in the dairy section at Eagle Supermarket.

"I haven't seen you in a while. How are you doing? How is Mom?"

"Mom's doing okay. She's adjusting."

"Rosemont's a nice place."

"Yeah, it definitely is. It's just that...I don't know..."

"I know. It's tough. It's hard seeing someone you love going through this. I know Mary was always so independent, especially after your dad died."

"Mmmm-hmmm. She's always been a strong person. To have to depend on other people, that's tough for her to accept."

Shirley grabbed Jacqui's hand. She could tell Jacqui was starting to tear up. "I know. I see it every day. You just do you best. That's all you can do."

"Are you still at Sugar Grove?"

"No, I left there about seven or eight months ago. I'm at SunnyHill now."

"Oh. We had Sugar Grove on our list when we were looking at nursing homes for Mom. "

"Right. I remember. They didn't have any openings."

"Tell me about it. God, we didn't know if we were ever going to find a good facility that actually had an opening."

"I know."

"I don't mean to pry, but can I ask you why you left Sugar Grove for SunnyHill?"

"You're not prying, honey. I just couldn't take all the politics anymore at Sugar Grove. I mean, Jesus, they were hiring so many younger girls. They were always complaining – always wanted time off. There was a lot of favoritism."

"Hmm. That's too bad."

"Yeah, SunnyHill is not Sugar Grove, or Rosemont, for that matter. But there's a lot less drama."

"Well, that's good."

"Not to mention, we actually have openings. In fact, we just recently had a guy come over from Rosemont. I couldn't believe it."

"Oh, really, I hadn't heard of anybody leaving Rosemont recently." Jacqui had not yet put the puzzle together.

"Well, he didn't stay with us very long. Poor Mr. Evans – having to deal with all those problems."

"Mr. Evans?"

Shirley put her hand over her mouth. "Oops, so much for privacy."

"My mom knows a "Mr. Evans". He's no longer at Rosemont. My mom wondered what happened to him."

"Gotta be the same guy."

"You said he's no longer there?"

"Yeah, I shouldn't say this, but what the hell, why stop now. He had to be rushed to the hospital."

"Do you know for what?"

"His kidneys are failing. Poor guy – he looked like he was in a lot of pain."

"Do you know what hospital?"

"I think it was St. Jude's."

"Thanks. Well, I should get going."

They hugged. "Please tell your mom I said hi. I'll have to come by and see her."

"She'd love that."

CHAPTER 61

Jennifer took Mary to 5:00 mass on Saturday. Afterwards they went to Marty's Restaurant. The weather was decent, and Mary was feeling pretty good. They got a table. They met Jacqui there.

"Hey." Jacqui arrived. She seemed hurried.

"Hi, honey."

"Hi, Mom, how are you feeling?"

"I'm doing okay today."

"Sorry I'm late."

"We just got some appetizers – cheese sticks and zucchini," Jennifer noted.

"Thanks. It's not bad out. I guess next weekend could be a different story, though."

"That's what I hear," Mary said. "I was watching the news. They are already calling for bad weather later next week."

"Well, I'm glad we got you out tonight, Mom," Jennifer said, as she dipped a cheese stick in some pizza sauce.

They were served pretty quickly. That was one of the things people liked about Marty's. Mary ended up eating a chicken sandwich and some of her fries. She always seemed to eat well at restaurants.

"Mom, I saw Shirley Thompson at the store."

"Really, I haven't seen her in a long time. How is she doing?"

"Ok. She's working at SunnyHill."

"SunnyHill?" Jennifer seemed surprised. "They're not exactly high on the list of quality nursing homes."

"I know. That's what I thought. She said she left Sugar Grove because of the drama."

"Huh. She'll get that no matter where she works."

"Anyways, she said a gentleman had recently come over to SunnyHill from Rosemont. She let it slip out that it was a "Mr. Evans.""

Mary stopped eating. "Do you think it's James Evans?"

"Who else could it be – from Rosemont?"

"Why would he go from Rosemont to SunnyHill?" Jennifer questioned. "He must have really wanted to get away from us."

"Well, Shirley said he had to be rushed to the hospital. He has a kidney that's failing, from what I understand."

Jennifer suddenly felt guilty about what she said.

There was less conversation after that. Mary experienced a rush of feelings again. What if James was dying? How much time did he have? Would there ever be resolution? So many unanswered questions.

CHAPTER 62

"What are you doing here?"

"Glad to see you, too." Anthony smiled.

"I'm sorry. It's good to see you. How did you know I was here?"

"I have connections, remember?"

"Oh, yea."

"So, what's going on? How are you feeling?"

"Not too well, they tell me. One of my kidneys is failing. I'm on dialysis. It's starting to affect other organs."

Anthony pulled the chair up to James' bed. James put his head back down on his pillow.

"I didn't think you'd be back in town so soon."

"My company has a large client in Pittsburgh. I had a meeting with them this morning. I got a rental car, and drove up here. I had heard you were sick."

"Does your mom know you're in town?"

"No."

James took a deep breath. He turned his head towards the window. He started crying. Anthony was caught off guard. His heart sank. "I'm scared," James said. "I don't want to die. There's so much unfinished business."

At that moment, Anthony wasn't sure what to say.

James continued. "I look back at my life. I've disappointed a lot of people. I disappointed myself. What would they call me – an underachiever? Christ, I had so much potential as a kid, and I pissed it all away. Oh, hell, no one's going to feel sorry for a sick, old man.

A nurse came into the room. 'Hello, how are you?"

"I'm fine, thank you," said Anthony.

'I'm sorry - Mr. Evans, we have to take you downstairs for a test."

"Oh, go ahead, I can leave," Anthony said.

"You don't have to," James replied. "This shouldn't take too long, should it?" James asked the nurse.

"Don't worry. No rush. I'll tell you what, I will call you later."

Anthony walked down the hall as James was led downstairs. At the nurses' station, a doctor was looking over a chart. He had a large cup of coffee in one hand. He caught Anthony out of the corner of his eye. Anthony seemed like he was walking aimlessly.

"Can I help you with anything?"

"Excuse me? Oh, I was just saying good-bye."

"Family member?"

"Yeah, I'm Mr. Evans' son."

"Anthony?"

"Yes."

"I feel like I know you, the way Mr. Evans has talked about you in the short time he's been here. I'm Dr. Benson."

They shook hands. "Nice to meet you, Doctor."

"They're just taking him down for some tests. Can we get you anything?"

Anthony was genuinely shocked. He hadn't met many doctors who went out of their way to see if visitors needed anything. This felt like something out of an old "Dr. Welby" program.

"No, I'm fine, thank you."

"I'm between rounds. Do you have a minute?"

There was a lounge area near the nurses' station. They sat down.

"So, how's he doing?"

Dr. Benson took a gulp of his coffee. Then he leaned forward, searching for the right thing to say.

"I'm going to be honest with you."

"Please."

"It's not good. His kidneys are failing, and it's starting to affect other organs. It looks like he's had this problem for quite some time. I mean, this didn't happen overnight. I don't think he took this too seriously early on. It's easy for me to say that – I haven't been in his position."

"At this point is there anything that can be done? Can dialysis and medications keep him going?"

"It can keep him going for a while, but..."

"But?"

"He really needs a new kidney. Without it, he'll die."

Anthony figured that's what he was going to say. But, those words still hit hard.

"I'm sorry. I wish I had better news."

"I know. I appreciate that."

"I'll tell you what – he sure speaks highly of you."

Anthony let out a little smile. "Thanks." That gave him a good feeling inside.

Dr. Benson's pager went out. "Gotta go. Take care of yourself."

Anthony sat back in his chair. He looked over to an elderly man sitting in the corner across the room. He was starring out the window. The man was hooked up to an oxygen tank. His chin was drawn. His hair was messed. He could barely keep his head up. He just looked beaten.

Anthony wondered how long this gentleman had to live. Did he know? Was he scared to die? Did he even want to keep living? Did he regret a lot of things in his life?

Anthony thought about James. James talked about missing opportunities in his life. It occurred to him that James was not necessarily afraid of dying – he was afraid of not living.....even at his age. A flood of emotions hit Anthony. He didn't just cry – he started bawling. Although he knew he was lucky to have had a good stepfather, James was his biological father. He gave him life. And he wondered what his life would have been. He felt worse for James. He seemed to have endured trial after trial in his life. He had to do something to help him.

CHAPTER 63

Jennifer and Jacqui met at Mary's room the following day.

"How did you sleep, Mom?"

"Oh, Jennifer, I couldn't stop thinking about James."

"I know what you mean. I feel badly for him."

"Do you think we should visit him?" Jacqui asked Jennifer.

"Do you think he'd want to see us? I mean, he left Rosemont. I'm assuming he wants to be alone."

Mary thought for a moment. "I'm not sure anyone really wants to be alone, Jennifer."

"I feel helpless," Jacqui noted.

"I know, honey. I'm not sure what we can do."

"I do!"

They all turned their heads. Anthony entered the room.

"Anthony, what are you doing here?" Mary asked.

"I had a meeting with a client in Pittsburgh. I got a rental and drove up."

"Well, that's nice. How long are you here?"

"I'm flying back tomorrow. I got my flight switched."

"We're glad you're here. We have some news for you," Jennifer said.

"About Mr. Evans?"

"Yeah, he's in the hospital."

"I know."

"How did you know?"

"Well, as I told Mr. Evans, I have some connections, and heard he was at St. Jude's."

"You saw him today," Mary asked.

"Yeah, I was only there for a short time."

"How is he?"

"Well, I had a chance to talk to his doctor. Anthony paused. "It's not good. Basically, if he doesn't get a new kidney...."

Mary's heart sank. She immediately thought back to when they were kids. He was such a strong, athletic kid. That now seemed like a lifetime ago.

There was silence for a moment.

"I want to help him," Anthony said. I decided I'm going to get tested...to see if I can donate one of my kidneys."

"What? Are you serious?" Jacqui asked.

"I am serious."

"Anthony, that's very noble of you, but think about what you are saying," Mary said.

"Yeah, do you really want to risk your own health?" Jennifer added.

"Girls, do you mind if I talk to your brother?"

"No problem," Jennifer said. "Jac, let's go down to the cafeteria."

"Come over here, honey." Mary was sitting in her recliner. Anthony sat on the edge of the bed.

"Anthony, what's going on?"

"What do you mean?"

"I mean, what's changed? I can't tell sometimes whether you're angry with him, or if you feel sorry for him. You really need to think about this."

"I guess –both. But I've done nothing but think since I found out my biological father was alive. I don't have illusions of grandeur here. It's not like we're going fishing and camping every weekend now. I know we may never get the opportunities to do a lot of things together, especially given the circumstances. But, it's not about that."

"Tell me, tell me what you are thinking. I just hope you're not doing this because of me. What he and I had existed many years ago – we can't relive the past – and you cannot reinvent it."

His mom might not have been the most educated person in the world, but she certainly had great wisdom and insight, Anthony thought to himself.

"We can't relive it, I know. But I might be in a position to do something. You know, for so much of my life I focused on myself and my job. I always had everything figured out."

"Honey, you were so independent and mature, even as a youngster. You earned everything you got, and have made a nice life for yourself."

Anthony looked out the window. 'I don't know. Maybe I can't put it into words. All I know is that I might have a chance to save a life – my biological father's life."

CHAPTER 64

Anthony flew home the following day. He had kept Lori updated regarding James' health. He hadn't told Lori of his plans. He'd have to do that face to face.

They were sitting in the family room. Lori was knitting a blanket. She had always been very crafty. She was "old school" as Anthony liked to say. She was a homebody. She was a great cook. She was able to balance working outside the home and running a household. Anthony knew he was very fortunate.

He watched her. He thought about how much she gave of herself to others. He wished he had been more like her.

"Who are you making that for?"

"It's for your mom. It's not real heavy material, so she'll be able to use it throughout the year."

"I thought it might be for her."

"How'd you know?"

"Cause' it's light blue."

"Yeah, I know she likes to wear things that are baby blue."

"I wanted to talk to you – it's about my visit to the hospital."

"What's up?"

"I've been thinking about this. I think I may be able to help James."

"How?'

"I am thinking maybe I'll get tested. Maybe I can donate one of my kidneys."

Lori immediately stopped knitting. "Are you serious?"

"Yes, I am being serious."

"Why?"

"What do you mean, why?"

"Well, I mean – he's older than you and he's lived a lot of his life."

"So his life has less value?"

"That's not what I meant."

"It's still a person's life, no matter what his age is."

"I know. But have you even thought about your own health?"

"I have been thinking about that. I know there are risks. But I wouldn't be the first one. They have been doing this surgery for years."

Lori put down the blanket and sat next to her husband. She grabbed his hand. "Honey, this is not like donating blood. This could be life altering. Have you thought about us – about Kristy? What if something would happen to you?"

"I know – for some reason I just feel very strongly about this."

Anthony squeezed her hand. He gave her a quick smile. She gave him a kiss on his forehead. It was late. She had had a long day and they would talk about this in the morning, she told him. She was heading to bed.

Anthony sat back on the couch and starred at the ceiling. "God, I know I haven't prayed much. I know I'm probably in no position to be asking for favors. But I need your help. My father needs your help."

CHAPTER 65

"Did you sleep well?"

"What do you think?" Lori asked Anthony.

"I guess I unloaded a bomb on you last night."

"You could say that."

Anthony was seated at the kitchen table.

"Do you want anything?" Lori asked.

"Well, if you're offering."

"I have some eggs in the fridge. I could scramble some."

"Sounds good. I made some coffee. You might just have to warm it up."

"I see that. Thank you."

Anthony was in his pajamas. He enjoyed Sunday mornings. He worked in a fast-paced environment all week, including some Saturdays. When Sunday arrived, he was ready to relax. He "slept in" until 7:30. Lori usually didn't get up until later on Sundays. Anthony enjoyed the quiet time.

Lori cracked some eggs and got breakfast going. She poured herself a cup of coffee. As she was beating the eggs, Anthony started the conversation.

"This is something I've been thinking about, Lori."

Lori didn't say anything at first. She poured the eggs into a frying pan. She finally spoke up.

"I don't know...something just doesn't feel right to me."

"What do you mean?"

She threw the towel down on the counter and turned to Anthony. "I guess I am trying to understand everything. You're willing to risk your life for someone you have mixed feelings for. Are you really doing this for James, or are you experiencing some kind of "bravado?"

"That's not fair. You think I'm trying to be some kind of superhero?"

"I'm sorry. I didn't mean it that way."

"It sure sounded like you did. You said it – you must have meant it."

Lori put the scrambled eggs on the kitchen table. A couple slices of bread popped up from the toaster.

Anthony helped himself to another cup of coffee. "You want a refill?"

"No, I'm good."

They both sat down and started eating.

"I don't want to argue," she noted.

"I don't want to argue, either. I don't know why everybody seems to be giving me so much grief."

Lori put down her piece of toast, and stared at Anthony. "Think about it. Just think about it. A year ago you didn't even know your biological father. Now you want to save his life."

Anthony got sarcastic. "You're right. Maybe I should let him die."

"Don't be a smart ass. You know what I mean."

Anthony took a deep breath and calmed down. "I can't explain it. I'm conflicted. Believe me. But, there is just something that is pushing me in this direction. I really can't explain it."

Lori sat back and took a sip of her coffee. She looked out the back window. "I'm proud of you for what you want to do. I really am. I'm…I'm just terrified that something might go wrong. My God – Kristy's still young. She needs a father that's going to be around."

"I understand. But they've been doing this surgery for years."

"It's not just the surgery. Have you thought about your life after the surgery? What about your quality of life? Will it be the same? What if you get really sick at some point – what problems are you going to face?"

"They're all valid questions. And believe me, I've thought about that. I just feel liked I am being called to do this. It's almost like a higher power is calling me to do this."

Lori knew she wasn't going to change his mind. Really, she wasn't necessarily trying to. She just wanted to make sure he was thinking this through. She was genuinely concerned about James. But, she was looking out for her husband and her daughter.

She was intrigued by Anthony's words. She had never heard him talk like that. He certainly hadn't been a particularly spiritual person. He was usually skeptical about such things. But she noticed he was changing. Some of his views seemed to be changing. His outlook seemed to be changing.

And, who knows – maybe he was being called by a higher power. If so, who was she to question it?

CHAPTER 66

Anthony went to work the next week and discussed the situation with his bosses. They were very understanding. Because he rarely used his vacation time, he had almost three months of vacation time built up.

They had a lot of the same concerns and questions that Mary and Lori had, especially the effect on Anthony's health. They were still a business, first and foremost. Anthony was a consistent top producer and they were not only concerned about him personally, but also the lost production that would have to be accounted for. But Anthony was a long term, loyal employee. They left the decision to him.

One day Anthony was sitting in his office. He was on a sales call when Peter Jansen came into his office. Peter was one of the top executives at the firm. Anthony ended his call.

"You didn't have to end the call. I could have come back."

"Oh, no problem. We were just finishing up." Anthony seemed perplexed as to why he had come by his office. While Anthony was in regular communications with some of the executives, he rarely talked to Peter. Peter closed the door behind him. Anthony could instantly feel the butterflies in his stomach. What was this about?

Peter sat down on the couch to the right of Anthony's desk. "How are things going?"

"Ok. Thanks." Anthony seemed genuinely confused.

Peter smiled. "I had heard you may be involved in a serious surgery."

Anthony cleared his voice. "Yes, I have been thinking about donating a kidney to my father. His health is failing."

Peter nodded his head.

"If this is a problem, I can certainly reconsider." Anthony didn't want to, but he thought perhaps that Peter was raising his objection to him being away from the office for an extended period. As it turned out, Anthony need not worry.

"Actually I know what you are going through. I thought I might be able to share some perspective."

"Ok."

"Many years ago, I had been to a few doctors. I was sick – off and on, you know. I was having pains around my intestines. Finally, one doctor ran an extended series of tests. They found out I was born with only one kidney."

Anthony looked surprised.

"Yeah, what are the odds? Anyways, my son comes to me and says he wants to give me one of his kidneys. I was stunned. I didn't know what to say. Well, after a lot of tears and soul searching, my wife and I agreed to it. We were very scared, obviously, for our son. We were concerned what his life would be like after the surgery."

"Wow! Everything turned out okay, I hope."

"Yes. He's doing well. I'm doing well. Certainly, there's always that fear. But, so far, so good.

"Thank you for sharing this with me."

"Well, I certainly admire what you are doing. It takes a lot of courage, and a lot of love."

"Thank you. I've thought about it for a while. I feel like I'm in a position to possibly help."

Peter got up from the couch. He put his hands in his pockets and looked down at the floor. "You know what's really amazing? Every time my son and I see each other, there's that split second where only we know what each other is thinking. We're forever connected. I mean, we're family, so we're connected. But there's a greater bond there that I just can't explain."

Anthony had made up his mind. He called Dr. Benson and explained what he was thinking. Dr. Benson asked that Anthony and Lori meet with him and some other doctors.

CHAPTER 67

Anthony and Lori flew to Erie, Pennsylvania. They picked up a rental car and drove to St. Jude's hospital.

After the initial meeting with Dr. Benson and some other physicians that had performed kidney transplants, Anthony went through some preliminary tests.

Anthony was exhausted, so they decided to go to their hotel.

The next day, they met with Dr. Gabriel Schuster. Dr. Benson was in surgery.

"Hello. How was your evening?"

"Good, thanks. I slept like a log," Anthony said.

"Tell me about it – he was snoring like crazy," Lori added.

Dr. Schuster laughed. "Well, so far things are looking good, but we'd like a run a couple more tests. Probably today and tomorrow. Is that okay?"

Anthony looked at Lori. "Ah, yes, we could do that. I just have to call the hotel to see if they can add another night or two."

"You don't have to worry about that. The hospital has a wing for families when there are extended stays, or if there are serious surgeries involved. We'll make sure you have a room."

"Thank you very much," Lori said.

"Anthony was then poked and prodded several more times. He was in a waiting area when Dr. Benson walked by.

"Hello. How are you doing today?"

"Not too bad."

"You probably feel like a pin cushion."

"I guess I was a little naïve about how much testing and how many procedures had to be done."

"Well, we'll finish up tomorrow. Did they talk to you about staying in our family wing?"

"Yes, we got everything worked out. Thank you."

"Great. Do you have any questions?"

"No, I think I'm good for now."

"Ok. I think that's it for today. Have you said anything to Mr. Evans?"

"No, I didn't want to say anything until I knew for sure."

"That's probably a good idea."

Dr. Benson started to walk away. "Hey Doc, thanks a lot."

"Thank you, the Doctor said, with an emphasis on "you."

CHAPTER 68

James was on the top floor of the hospital. There was a very spacious lounge area. He was looking out the large window.

"They told me that I could find you here."

James turned quickly. "Whoa, you surprised me."

"I'm full of surprises lately."

"You keep showing up when I least expect you too."

"They said you like coming up here."

"Yeah, they're putting up a building across the street. I like watching them."

Anthony looked out the window. "Wow."

"I know. I don't know how many stories. They keep adding."

"What are they putting there? Do you know?"

"They are going to put the oncology and cardiology divisions there. A lot of the specialists will be located there."

Anthony pushed one of the cushion chairs closer to James.

"Are you on a business trip again?"

"Actually, no. I'm here for something much more important. I...I've been going through a lot of tests. I'm staying in the hospital family wing."

James looked confused but didn't say anything.

Anthony leaned towards James. "The doctors told me how serious your condition is. I have been thinking about this for a while. I want to give you one of my kidneys."

James didn't say anything at first. His jaw dropped. "Oh, I can't let you do that."

"I want to."

"Anthony, I'm an old man. You have your whole life ahead of you."

"You still have your life ahead of you," Anthony iterated.

"The way I feel now – to be honest – I wish I was dead."

"You don't have to feel that way. I can help. I want to help."

He looked at Anthony. "Why would you want to help me? What have I done for you?"

"I don't know. I guess...because you're my father."

James started to cry. They both realized it was the first time Anthony directly referred to him as his father.

Anthony then broke down in tears. He let out a laugh at the same time. "Do I need any more reason than that?"

James started to laugh, in between a couple coughs. "Look at us – a couple of sad saps, wouldn't you say?"

They embraced.

CHAPTER 69

After more discussions between James, Mary, Anthony and Lori, things started moving quickly. Anthony would come back soon for the actual operation. It would take place at a larger hospital in Pittsburgh that was better equipped to handle this type of surgery.

CHAPTER 70

"She died?" Mary was devastated.

"I'm really sorry, Mary," Hanna said.

Erma had passed on. It appeared that she might have suffered a stroke. She went to bed the previous night, but didn't wake up this morning.

Mary didn't feel like eating breakfast. She stayed in her room. She may not have known Erma very long, but they got very close. They were best friends at Rosemont. Frankly, it was Mary's closest friend she had in years.

She felt very alone. It felt like her first day at Rosemont.

It wasn't such a shock that a resident would die. It was estimated that one resident died every three months. Just as quickly a new resident would move into that person's room.

But, why Erma? She was the one person Mary could talk to. Mary had told Erma the story about James and her. She opened up to Erma about so many things from her past. Erma never judged. She was a great sounding board. Erma once told Mary that the love Mary and James experienced as kids was the same kind of love Erma enjoyed with her husband for many years.

CHAPTER 71

Jennifer and Jacquie went with Mary to the funeral home. Montgomery's Funeral Home was close to Rosemont.

The viewing would be that Sunday, from 2:00 p.m. to 6:00 p.m. A private service would be held afterwards for immediate family only.

There weren't too many people there. It seemed like a majority of them were some of the nurses and aides from Rosemont. That wasn't surprising. Erma was very well liked at Rosemont. She never gave anybody any problems.

Mary could overhear Erma's children talking. "She looks very pretty," one lady said to Erma's oldest daughter, Valerie.

"Yes, thanks. She always loved that pink sweater," Valerie said.

What the hell? Mary thought to herself. *She always liked that pink sweater? No, she didn't.* Mary wanted to tell everyone. She just got that sweater as a Christmas gift from her son, Jeffrey. She didn't even care much for pink. Purple was her favorite color.

Speaking of Jeffrey, she could hear him speaking to an elderly couple. "Mom hadn't been at the nursing home long. She adjusted well though. She loved sitting next to the pond, feeding the geese."

"Sounds like she was doing okay, then," the gentleman said.

"Yeah. Things worked out. She had made it clear she did not want to move in with any of us. She was very stubborn."

Mary wanted to vomit. First of all, they were not permitted to feed the geese at the pond. Secondly, she didn't want to move in with any of the children because they never asked! Erma had confided in Mary that she was very hurt that none of her children wanted to be burdened.

Mary made her way up to the coffin. She leaned over and touched Erma's hands. Erma was holding a rosary that Mary had given her. Mary won it at a game of bingo at Rosemont. Erma had mentioned that she didn't have one. Mary also noticed a few photos of Erma when she was younger. Even after all these years, she still had a youthful face. There was a photo of Erma with her husband. It looked like they may have been in their 30's. They were standing in front of a Christmas tree. Her husband was tickling her. It looked like they were very happy.

Mary laughed to herself. In the photo, Erma was wearing a full-length dress. Her husband was wearing sweat pants, with a sweatshirt and ball cap. Erma had said that they were complete opposites. The foods they ate; the clothes they wore; some of their interests – they just seemed so different. But they got along so well. Erma mentioned that they had rarely argued. They allowed each other to be individuals.

"You must be Jeffrey," Mary said to Erma's son.

"Yes." They shook hands. Mary noticed it was not a very firm handshake.

Mary tried to say something that you would normally say in such a situation. "Your mom and I became close friends at Rosemont. She was very proud of her family."

"Oh, thank you. Thank you for coming."

That was it. Mary and the girls made their way to the car. The girls decided to take Mary to Everett's restaurant, since they were already out.

After a few minutes of silence in the car, Jennifer decided to start the conversation. "Well, Erma's family seems nice."

"They're assholes," Mary said quickly.

Jennifer and Jacqui looked at each other.

"O-o-okay," Jacqui said. "Tell us how you really feel, Mom."

"I'm sorry for that...but what a farce. Did you hear them talking about Erma?"

"I know. I agree," Jacqui said. "I was just trying to be nice."

"They're full of shit. "I'm sorry. I apologize again."

The girls laughed.

"They didn't know their mother. Pink sweater – are you kidding me? I think she may have worn that sweater once." Mary put her right hand over her forehead. "I think I knew her better than they did. They hardly visited."

"You were definitely closer to Erma," Jacqui said.

"Did Erma ever talk about her children?" Jennifer asked. "Was she upset that they didn't visit much?"

"Well, I'll tell you. Every once in a while she would talk about them, but she would stop. You could tell it hurt her that they didn't visit much or call much, for that matter. The few times they did visit, she was always very appreciative."

"That's a shame."

"It really is. She deserved so much more from them. I'll say this – she did talk about her husband. It sounded like they enjoyed a really nice marriage."

"See how lucky you are," Jennifer joked.

"Oh, honey, I realize it. I'm so fortunate."

"I was just kidding, Mom."

"No, you're right. I'm lucky to have such caring children who are always there for me."

"You know the saddest part," Jennifer added. "You would think that after their father died, they would have learned. I mean, they had an opportunity to spend time with Erma. She's gone now. They'll never get that chance again."

Those words hit Mary hard. Jennifer was exactly right. Erma's kids had an opportunity to spend as much time as they could with their mom. It's an opportunity that many others don't get. They blew it. They'll never get that back. *Maybe one day they'll realize that*, Mary thought. She hoped.

If Mary learned anything from Erma's passing, it reaffirmed her belief that she and James had been given an opportunity at a second chance – so had James and Anthony. They could not take that for granted.

CHAPTER 72

Anthony and Lori drove to Highland Hospital in Pittsburgh. For such a long trip, there wasn't too much conversation, relatively speaking. They were both very nervous. Anthony was scared. He might have not said it, but he was. It was actually starting to sink in that something could go terribly wrong – for him or for James.

He thought about Kristy. If something happened to him, would she see him as someone who was trying to save a life, or someone who made a decision that would dramatically alter his own family's life?

But he was also confident. He believed it was the right thing to do. Regardless of how it happened, James was also his family.

Jennifer and Jacqui drove Mary to the hospital. Mary was certainly concerned for James. But she couldn't stop thinking about Anthony. What if something happened to him? After all, she had the choice to tell him about his biological father. No one forced her. She thought about that on the drive down. Had she kept things a secret no one would be going through this right now. In that sense, she was feeling guilty.

As they drove down Interstate 79, Mary noticed the signs along the way. There were exits for places like Rexford, Butler and Mars. She recalled James playing football against these teams when they were in high school. After most games, on Friday nights, Mary would sit cross-legged on the edge of her bed, with the radio on. She liked having just one night light on. That was her time – her time to dream about Jimmy and what the future would hold. She once told James that she would give him a son -and he would grow up to play football - just like his dad. They would be pals, friends, and "teammates." And now, James and his son were teaming up for something much more.

CHAPTER 73

Anthony and Lori arrived at the hospital, shortly after Mary and the girls arrived. The family was briefed on the details of the operation. They had heard this all before, but it had to be repeated. There were many forms to review – many pre-surgery waivers to sign.

Mary, Jennifer, Jacqui and Lori would be staying in one of the hospital housing units for family members. Their unit was within walking distance – at least for the girls. It was spacious, and had more amenities than some higher-priced rentals.

Jennifer took it all in. "No wonder health care costs have skyrocketed."

It was a good icebreaker to relieve all the tension.

After getting settled, they went back to the hospital. They sat at one end of the cafeteria. The girls had picked up a couple pizzas at Vito's, which was right down the road from the hospital. It was the old style Italian pizza – large thin slices with lots of grease.

Anthony ate very well. Mary could tell he was nervous. When he was a boy, he would eat very quickly when he was nervous, or had a problem. She looked at him. It took her back thirty-some years. At dinnertime, Anthony would sit in his usual chair at the back of the kitchen table. Usually he was the last one finished. He was very deliberate. But if something was on his mind, he would eat quickly and asked to be excused.

She took hold of Anthony's hand. "It's going to be okay."

They stopped eating. Anthony looked at Mary, and smiled. He knew exactly what Mary was referring to. It put him at ease, at least for the moment.

Dr. Kevin Richards walked by. He was carrying a coffee and croissant. He would take the lead in tomorrow's surgery.

"How's everybody tonight, folks?"

"Hello, Doctor," Mary said.

"I think we're all a little nervous," Jennifer added.

"I know. That is certainly understandable. But believe me; I am going to have some of the most experienced surgeons and nurses with me tomorrow morning. I am very confident."

That made everyone feel a little better.

But just when he tried looking at his watch, he spilled some of his coffee on himself. "Ah, shit, dammit." He looked up at everyone, staring at him. "Sorry for my language. This is not the first time I've ruined a good shirt by spilling coffee."

Jacqui quickly gave him a bunch of napkins. He was wiping his shirt when he started to giggle. Then everyone else started laughing. "Believe me folks; I handle a scalpel better than a cup of coffee."

CHAPTER 74

While Mary and the girls went back to the housing unit, Anthony went to James' room. They were continuing to find that they had more in common than they originally thought. They watched reruns of "Happy Days," "Family Ties," and "Wonder Years." Afterwards they played several games of 500 Rummy.

Anthony looked at his watch. "Well, it's getting late. I should head back to my room and get to bed."

"Yeah, I hear you have a big day tomorrow," James quipped.

"That's funny – I heard the same about you."

"Have a good night. Get some rest."

"Okay, Dad, you do the same."

James wasn't sure if Anthony realized it, but he called him "dad." It made him feel really good.

James sat back on his bed. The lights were turned off. The only light was from near the door, coming from the hallway. It got very quiet. He thought about how he got here, and wondered what lie ahead. He thought about Mary and Anthony.

Anthony was lying in his bed with the lights turned off. He thought about how he got here, and what may lie ahead. He looked out the window at the city lights. He thought about James and his mom.

Mary was back at the housing unit. The girls had helped her get ready for bed. The lights in her room were turned off but there was a light on in the living room. She could barely hear the girls talking. She tightly held on to her rosary. She thought about how she got here, and what may lie ahead. She thought about Anthony and James.

CHAPTER 75

James and Anthony were prepped for surgery. Dr. Richards provided a final overview. It would be a long surgery.

The surgery got underway very early. Mary and the girls sat in one of the large waiting rooms. There were several TV's, and area for puzzles and games, and a few computers. After sitting there for a few hours, the girls thought it would be a good idea to get Mary out of the hospital for a while. There was a mall nearby. They provided a couple of the nurses with their cell numbers, in order to receive any updates.

Lori was dealing with a bad headache, and decided to stay at the hospital. They allowed her to lie down in a small room not far from the operating area.

Mary and the girls walked through several stores. There wasn't much conversation. They had been there a while when they decided to get something to eat. They walked to the food court and ordered. It felt good to sit down. They were not yet done eating when Jennifer received a call on her cell phone.

"Hello."

"Hello, Jennifer? This is Colleen Meyer."

"Who is it?" Jacqui asked, impatiently.

"Shhh," Jennifer whispered. "It's Colleen Meyer."

"This is Jennifer."

"The nurses' station said you were at the mall."

"Yes, we're just finishing eating. How are things going?"

She paused. "Well, we've run into a problem."

"What problem?"

Jacqui stood up. She wanted to take the phone, but Jennifer wasn't giving it up.

"It would be better if we could talk in person," Colleen stated.

"Ok, we're on our way."

"What did she say?" Jacqui asked.

"She said there were some problems."

Mary didn't say anything. She simply stared at the table. Something had happened to James.

"Come on, we have to get going," Jennifer said, somewhat frantically.

They got to the car and raced to the hospital.

"This is my fault."

"What? What are you talking about, Mom?" Jacqui asked.

"If I had just kept my past where it was supposed to stay – in the past – we wouldn't be in this position right now. And now something's happened to Mr. Evans."

"Mom, it's nobody's fault," Jennifer said, trying to reassure her.

When they got to the hospital, they went back to the waiting room to meet Colleen. They hadn't been there a couple minutes when Dr. Richards walked towards them.

Mary noticed him first.

"Hi, Doctor, Colleen told us there was a problem?" Jennifer said.

"It might be better if we talk in private. We can use the room where Lori was resting."

They felt incredibly guilty. In all the excitement, they forgot about calling Lori.

They got to the room. Lori was sitting up on the bed, rubbing her eyes.

"How are you feeling honey?" Mary asked.

"A little better. What's going on?"

Dr. Richard intervened. "The surgery had been going fairly smoothly, but then we encountered a problem."

"Is James okay? Was the surgery too much for him?'

Dr. Richards looked towards Lori. "All indications – and it's very, very early – are that James is okay. It's actually Anthony. We've had some complications."

Lori jumped from the bed. "What do you mean?"

"We started having problems getting his blood pressure under control. Once the kidney was out, it's as if his body initially reacted negatively."

"Can I see him?" Lori asked.

"As the pressure seemed to drop further, he lapsed into a coma."

"A coma?" Lori put her hands over her face. Jacqui went over to try to console her.

"Right now we're trying to keep his vitals stable. He certainly has a good chance of coming out of the coma."

"A chance?" Lori yelled. She started crying.

"I don't understand," Jennifer said. "I thought you said this was a pretty common surgery."

"No, we didn't say there was anything routine about this. It's still a transplant. Now, we have an excellent team monitoring the situation."

Lori had her right hand over her forehead. Her headache had come back in multiples. She sat down on a couch. Jennifer sat next to her, and put her arm around her.

Mary spoke up. "Is my son going to die?"

Dr. Richards knelt next to Mary. "I promise you that we will do everything we can to provide Anthony with the best care."

It didn't answer her question.

Dr. Richards patted her hand. "I have to check on Anthony and James."

"I want to see my husband," Lori said loudly.

"Of course."

"Lori, why don't you and Mom go," Jacqui suggested.

"Yeah, that's probably a good idea," Jennifer added.

Mary and Lori entered Anthony's room. Interestingly, Mary seemed like the stronger one. Lori immediately began to cry. She ran her hand through Anthony's hair.

"Why don't you sit down, honey," Mary said.

Lori pulled the chair closer to his bed. She touched his face. Mary put her hand on Lori's shoulder.

"Oh, I'm sorry, Mom, you should sit down."

"No, please. It seems like all I do is sit." Mary pulled some tissues from her pocket, and gave them to Lori.

"Thank you. You had them in your pocket?"

"I've been doing a lot of crying lately."

They stared at Anthony's face. It had a little bit of color. He didn't look as bad as they had expected. But, his body was stiff. If it weren't for the all machines you would have thought he was dead.

"I'm so very sorry, Lori." Mary started crying extremely hard.

"For what, Mom? You didn't do anything."

"Yes....yes I did. Looking back, I should have kept my past with James a secret. I guess it's true what they say – some things are better left unsaid. Now look what I have caused."

"Don't even talk like that. Things happen for a reason. Anthony is supposed to save James' life."

"But what if it costs him his own life?"

CHAPTER 76

After Jennifer and Jacqui spent some time with Anthony, they took Mary to the hospital chapel. Mary just wanted to be alone.

It was more like a church than a chapel. It had many old features – old statutes, stained glass windows, and a lot of oak. It seemed to be out of place compared to the continuous updates and renovations in the main hospital.

She sat in the back pew. She took out her rosary. Ironically, it finally occurred to her that she received this rosary from the funeral home when her husband had died. She always kept it in her purse. And she took her purse everywhere she went. And here she was...using that very same rosary to ask God to let her son live, and for James to accept his new kidney. It was a lot to ask. She knew that. She learned a long time ago that you rarely get what you want. But praying made her feel better. She tried to reason with God to give her family a second chance.

A gentleman walked in and sat in the back of the chapel, to Mary's left. She looked over to him. He smiled. She did the same. He could see that Mary had been crying. Her face was red. He walked over to her.

"Excuse me, I don't mean to bother – is everything alright?"

"Oh, yes. I'm just getting my prayers in. You're not bothering me. Please sit down. I'm Mary."

"I'm Dr. Montgomery. Thank you. You must have a family member at the hospital?"

"Yes. My son....and his father."

"Oh, my. Is everything okay?"

"Well, they just went through a kidney transplant. I guess things were going well. But, they had some kind of complication, and my son is now in a coma."

"I'm sorry to hear that. I can tell you there are excellent doctors and nurses in that area – I am sure they are doing everything they can."

"Oh, yes, I don't doubt that. I just wish there was something I could do to fix this."

The doctor's face seemed perplexed. Even Mary picked up on it.

"My son, Anthony, and his father were reunited not too long ago. It's because of me. It's a long story."

"Oh, I think I get the picture. You are feeling somewhat guilty."

"Yes. You're very perceptive, and very smart. That's probably why you're a doctor."

He laughed. "You shouldn't feel guilty. People make their choices. I am sure they were at peace with their decision to go ahead with the operation."

"They were. My son, especially. I had never seen him like that. He had every reason to hate me and his father, but ended up being so eager to help."

"Hmmm. The human spirit is an amazing thing."

"All I can do is sit here and pray. I don't know any other way I can help. I've been praying so much to Saint Anthony lately. He's the patron saint of lost things. Most people think that means physical things that are lost. But, I've been praying for something much deeper. I feel like my family has been lost, and now this was supposed to be a second chance."

Dr. Montgomery let her continue talking.

"I know there are no guarantees, but they sure sounded like they were confident about the surgery. They said they had a lot of experienced doctors and nurses involved. "

"Well, I'll tell you – that's one of the reasons I like coming in here. I just ask God to keep giving me the grace and strength to continue doing what I love."

"What is it that you love?"

"I love helping people. That's why I became a doctor. I wanted to see people getting better. I wanted to have an effect."

"You sure sound like a very fine doctor."

He laughed. "Thank you. But, I'm only one part, though. You know, people will tell me that I helped save their loved ones, or did something to change their lives. But, it's really God. I truly believe that God works through me. That's why I continue to ask Him for His grace to allow me to continue doing what I am doing. But ultimately, it's in His hands."

He continued. "I guess what I'm saying is that you just have to really put your trust in God. Just continue to pray…and believe."

"Thank you. You know you would have made an excellent priest, as well."

"Funny you should say that. My mother wanted me to become a priest. She was very religious. She thought we needed a priest in the family."

"How about your father?"

"My dad? He really didn't care. He was a simple man. He just loved the casinos and playing the ponies. That's probably why my mom thought we needed a priest in the family."

He got Mary to laugh. She felt better. He made her feel like things were going to be okay.

Before he left, Dr. Montgomery knelt in front of a statue. There were several lit candles in front. She couldn't tell but it looked like he put something in front of the statue.

Lori and one of the nurses came in to check on Mary. "How ya' doin', honey?" the nurse asked.

"Oh, okay, I guess. Talking to that nice doctor made me feel a little better. "

"Dr. Montgomery? Yeah, he's a great doctor. "

"Where does he work?"

"He works with the younger cancer patients. "

"Wow, that's got to be tough," Lori noted.

"Sure is. That's who he likes to work with, though."

"It sounds like he visits the chapel often," Mary said.

"Well, every time a new cancer patient arrives, he comes in here to pray. Then he puts a white flower at the base of the Mary statue. He says it's a symbol of hope. I've never met any doctor like him. He's almost God-like..."

The nurse left.

"Well, Mom, are you hungry?" Lori asked.

"Yeah, I guess I could use a sandwich. How are you holding up, dear?"

Lori sat down next to her. She started crying. "Sorry – all I have been doing is crying."

Mary took hold of her hands. "I think things are going to be okay. I feel a real presence in this chapel. I can't explain it."

"You think God heard your prayers?"

Mary thought about her conversation with Dr. Montgomery. "I think he is listening now."

Mary was tired and decided to use her wheelchair. They went to the little café near the main entrance to the hospital. They ordered a couple of deli sandwiches.

"My, this place is busy," Mary observed.

"It sure is."

They sat for a while. They ate slowly, watching people entering and leaving the hospital. They wondered why they were here, and which of their loved ones was in the hospital. Was it serious? How many were experiencing the pain and sorrow that they were experiencing?

They checked on Anthony. There was no change. They were not permitted to see James yet, but were receiving updates. James had been in and out – he was very groggy and tired. It would be a while before he was fully awake.

It was late. They went back to the hospital housing unit. It had been a very long day.

CHAPTER 77

Lori's cell phone rang loudly. She had it set on the highest level. She jumped from the bed.

The only light in the room was from her phone. It read "4:25."

"Hello."

"Ah, yes, this is Joanne Morris, from the hospital."

"Yes, this is Lori – Anthony's husband."

"Ma'am, sorry to call at this time, but you and your family will want to come to the hospital."

"Oh my God, what happened? Did something happen to Anthony? Did something happen to James? Her voice was getting louder. She heard the light switch go on in Jennifer's bedroom.

"Oh, no ma'am. It's your husband – he's awake."

Lori instantly started crying. She felt a lump in her throat fall to her stomach. It was instant relief and joy. "Oh my God...thank you so much...thank you..."

"You're very welcome. We'll see you soon."

"We'll be right there."

There was a knock on Lori's bedroom door. "Lori, are you alright?"

Lori ran to the door, and opened it as fast as she could. She gave Jennifer a big hug. "He's awake! Anthony's awake!"

By then Jacqui and Mary had awoken. They ran into Mary's room to tell her the great news.

Mary started crying as well. She pulled her right arm from underneath her blankets. She was clutching her rosary tightly. She looked at the rosary. "Thank you, Lord. Thank you for listening." She also believed her late husband was listening.

They changed quickly and headed to the hospital. As busy as the hospital was seven or eight hours ago, it was exceptionally quiet at this hour.

Joanne Morris was at the nurses' station. Lori ran up to her and gave her a hug.

They went in to see Anthony. A nurse was there, taking some vitals. She told Anthony there were some people who wanted to see him.

"Hey, how do you feel?" Lori asked, as she gave him a kiss and put her hand on top of this head.

"Hey," he replied, in a weak voice. "It's good to see you. It's good to see all of you."

Mary held his hand. "I thought we lost you. Oh, God, I don't know what I would have done."

"You didn't get rid of me yet." Anthony looked at Jacqui and Jennifer. He then looked back at Lori. "Wow."

"What?" Lori asked.

"Well, it's obvious you guys rushed over here – you don't have any makeup on. I probably look better than you guys right now."

They all laughed. "And to think we were worried about this guy," Jennifer quipped.

"How do you feel?" Lori asked.

"I feel okay. I'm sore. I don't know what happened. They said my pressure went down."

"We're just glad you made it. You gave us all a huge scare."

"How is James?"

"We haven't been allowed to see him yet. They said he's been in and out. Probably pretty well medicated, you know?"

Doctor Richards came into the room. "Good morning. Good to see our patient is awake."

"Wow, Doctor, are you working late...or working early?" Lori inquired.

"Both, I guess. I was supposed to leave after surgery last night but it got late, and I wanted to check on Anthony and James. I ended up getting a couple of hours of sleep here."

"How is James, Doc?" Anthony asked.

"So far, things are looking okay. We're monitoring some things, and because of his age, there are always risk factors. But so far, so good."

"Oh, by the way, I was asked to give this to you." He handed a note to Mary. She opened it and read it:

"Mary, before I left I went to check on your son. They said he came out of the coma. That's great news. Saint Anthony must be watching. See, the power is in the prayer. Best Wishes, Dr. Anthony Montgomery."

Mary clutched the note and smiled.

"Who's that from, Mom?" Jacqui asked.

"Oh, it's from a new friend..."

CHAPTER 78

Mary had to admit to herself that her feelings for James continued to get stronger. It wasn't that she was just worried about him. It was more than that. She had been getting closer to him, and she was sure James felt the same way. She had held on to the fact that she was a widow. Whether she liked it or not, that's how she was labeled.

With so many changes in her life, she was thinking differently. She looked at Anthony. He literally put his life on the line for his biological father. His life was changing and so was James' life. Mary was beginning to think she had put her life on hold for many years. Maybe it was time to make some changes. Looking at her son, she realized that you are never too old to grow and to change.

CHAPTER 79

After a couple days, Anthony was feeling better. He said he could feel himself get a little stronger.

Mary and Lori were permitted to see James. They entered his room. It was dark. He didn't hear them enter. "Hello, Mr. Evans, how are you?" Lori asked.

He slowly turned his head. He still seemed a little groggy. His words were a little slurred. "Oh, it's good to see you."

Lori grabbed his left hand. "They told us you've been in and out. But, it looks good so far. You must be a very strong man."

James made a crooked smile. "I'm not as strong as you think. They have to keep pumping me with drugs."

Mary stepped up to his bed. "Oh, Mary, I didn't even see you."

"How are you doing, old man?"

James let out a gruff laugh. "I'm better now." He was trying to say more but the words weren't easy.

"Here, drink some of this." Mary gave him a cup of ice water with a straw.

"Cold beer?"

"Ha, keep dreaming. It's ice water."

He took a couple big gulps. "Ah...that tastes good. So, is Anthony doing okay?"

Mary paused before speaking. "Well, he had some..."

Lori jumped in. "He's doing very well. He said he can't wait to see you."

"Oh, that's great. I knew we'd make it through this."

Lori had grabbed Mary's arm. Mary knew what Lori was doing, and she was right. There was no reason to tell James about Anthony falling into a coma. There was no need to upset him.

A nurse came into the room. "Mr. Evans, are you ready? We're going to take you down to x-ray. We want to take a look at what's going inside that body of yours."

"We'll come by later, Mr. Evans," Lori said. "You just take care of yourself."

Lori and Mary checked on Anthony. He was sleeping peacefully. They didn't want to bother him.

They headed back to the housing unit. "Mom, I'm going to drop you off and then go to the store to pick up some things."

"Oh, that would be great."

Lori helped Mary get situated in her room. Jacqui and Jennifer were out.

"I think I've got to get some groceries. We could use a nice, big meal tomorrow. I'll be back."

Mary put her hands on Lori. "Thank you, honey." She started getting a little emotional. "I always knew that Anthony was very fortunate to have found someone like you. You're a rock. You're an important part of this family. I love you more and more."

Lori broke up a little bit. "Mom, you know you're important to me, too. I've always admired how strong you are. Your strength has been an inspiration for me."

Lori paused. "Wow, let's quit blubbering. Let me pick up some groceries."

As Lori walked toward the door, she turned to Mary. "You're right, though. Anthony was very lucky to find me..."

CHAPTER 80

Mary, Lori, Jennifer and Jacqui went back to the hospital later that night. They sat with Anthony for a while. Dr. Richards said things were looking up. He certainly was not out of the woods, but he was starting to turn the corner.

They checked on James. He was resting comfortably. He was under a lot of medications, of course.

Mary sat down on a large rocker/recliner next to James' bed. She reclined the chair back. She said she was feeling tired. The past several days had taken a lot out of her, as well. The girls put a blanket over her.

"Do you think they'd let me stay here? I hate the thought of getting up and going back to the unit tonight."

"I don't know, Mom," Jacqui said. "I could ask."

"Are you sure you will be comfortable here?" Jennifer asked.

"It feels good. I'm actually very comfortable here."

They checked, and as far as the nurses were concerned, they didn't see any problem with Mary staying. They assured the girls they would assist Mary.

A light near the door way was left on. Otherwise it was dark in the room. It was very quiet. It was just Mary and James.

"So, how are you feeling, James?"

"I don't want to get too confident, but I feel a little better each day."

"That's a very good sign. I was so worried about you and Anthony."

"Is he doing as well as they say? I can't wait to talk to him."

Mary knew to take a cue from Lori. "Yes, he seems to be doing well. He's getting better each day – just like you."

"Oh, that's good to hear."

Mary reflected. "You know, that's our son lying in the other room. My God, when we were kids, who would have thought we would be here tonight. Life can be so strange."

James looked at her, and then turned his head. He stared up at the ceiling. "Do you remember our first dance?"

"How could I forget? We were at Harley's. I was hoping so much that you would ask me out. What made you think of that now?"

"Believe it or not, I actually thought we would end up together – even though it was only our first dance. There was just something about you. You were so different from the other girls. You were real. There was nothing fake about you."

James seemed to get a little chocked up. He fought it back. Mary noticed. "Mary, I had it all. I had college, I had football, and most importantly, I had a future with you. I can live with the mistakes I've made with college...but I can never forgive myself for walking away from you and Anthony."

"We can't do anything about the past. The important thing is what we have now. I'm here now. And our son is here now."

They held hands. They stopped talking. They ended up both falling asleep. Their hands never left each other.

CHAPTER 81

James and Anthony continued to improve, and were eventually cleared to go home. They never told James about Anthony lapsing into a coma.

Anthony and Lori went back to Boston. Kristy was so glad to see them. Because of school, she couldn't take that much time off and try to make up the work. She had stayed with her best friend, Amanda Byers. Amanda's parents, Tim and Vicky Byers were very good friends with Anthony and Lori. At first Kristy found it exciting staying there. But as the novelty wore off, she couldn't wait to be reunited with her own family.

James and Mary were fortunate enough to have their rooms still reserved at Rosemont. The fact is, many nursing homes would have filled their rooms after being away for a certain time period. But that was another reason Rosemont set itself apart from other facilities. Rosemont took James back with open arms.

As the days passed, James and Mary became closer. Both sensed it. They spent most of their days watching movies together and playing cards.

James was doing remarkably well. There would always be a concern, especially at his age. But, he encountered very few complications.

One night James brought a box with him to Mary's room.

"What's that?'

"You know, I didn't end up with many personal possessions, but I always kept this box with me."

James dumped the box onto her bed.

"You kept old photos?"

"I sure did. It never even occurred to me that there would be some photos of us."

They started glancing through them. Mary sighed deeply. "The girls...look at them."

"Yeah, the "Hearts", right?"

"Yes, the "Hearts". Look at Rhonda Sue. Look how young she looked. This was taken at Harley's, wasn't it?"

"Yep – see the jukebox in the background?"

"Speaking of young, look at you," James said, as he handed another photo to her."

"Oh, what a nice picture. Look how great we looked." It was a picture of Mary and James after one of his games. Their smiles showed a young couple very much in love."

"Oh, look at this one," Mary said.

"My God, look at all the hair we had." It was a photo of James, Stevie, Lenny and Jerry. They were sitting on the front hood of James' car. "I remember Stevie always had that leather jacket."

"Ahhh."

"What?"

Mary picked up a photo and gave it to James. It was a picture of James and his mom.

"Wow. This was at my high school graduation."

"She was very proud of you."

"Yeah, she was a good person. We didn't have much, but she never made me feel that way. She worked so hard."

"Look at this one, James. You're dressed in uniform."

"Hmm. I was on my way to boot camp."

"Whatever happened then? How did you end up going into the Army?"

James sat back. She could tell these were painful memories, but he had never talked about them.

"Boy, I don't know. I guess after your father told me you were not keeping the baby, I just kind of lost it. I guess I took that as a sign that you did not want to see me." Before Mary could say anything, he spoke quickly. "I know that was dumb of me, but I didn't know what to think. I never went to Ohio University. I felt so guilty at the time, that I wasn't even thinking straight. I couldn't even think about college then. I think I really enlisted just to get away. I figured that gave me a reason to leave -- as if it justified everything."

"After I served for a couple years, I didn't know what to do when I came back. I felt just as lost then. No job, no money. I ended up doing odd jobs until I got employed in a factory."

"I didn't stop thinking about you, though. I want you to know that. It probably would have been a lot easier if I was able to get you out of my head, but that was just not possible."

"I had always wondered what happened. I mean I used to follow football some, but I never heard whether you were actually playing for Ohio University. My friends quickly scattered within a year or two after high school. I felt alone. Even though my parents were helping me raise Anthony, I felt very alone."

"I am so sorry for that."

"I know you are. I'm sorry, too."

"It must have been extremely difficult, especially at that time."

"Well, there was always rumors and gossip. I could literally hear people talking about me behind my back. I eventually came to the conclusion that talking about me made other people feel better about their own lives. And, my parents! God, my father almost disowned me at first. It took him a long time to come to grips with it. I don't think he ever forgave me. I could always count on my mom. Her motherly instincts took over, and she helped me in so many ways."

They held each other's hands.

"Well, one very important thing came from all of this ---- our son. He was, and is, a special gift, and I would have never thought of giving him up."

"He is a special person, isn't he? He takes after his mom..."

CHAPTER 82

The staff had noticed that James' disposition changed upon his return to Rosemont. He didn't have the constant physical pains. Even more, it seemed like his emotional pain had started to subside. He and Mary were spending a lot of time together. It was a healing process for both. And they both were looking toward their futures.

CHAPTER 83

"Hey, you guys ready?"

"I think we're getting there," Jennifer told Anthony.

"Everything okay?"

"Oh, you can imagine what it's like, trying to get them going," she said, referring to James and Mary.

Anthony smiled. He was glad he was in Boston. "Well, he'll definitely be surprised. I can't wait to see his face."

"If we don't kill them before we get there," Jennifer said.

"Ha ha. I'll tell you what. When you get here, you can sit back and relax. We'll take it from there."

"That sounds like a plan. But we won't be sitting back. We can't wait to see the sights of Boston."

"Well, there's plenty to see."

"Can't wait. Well, I better get them going so we can get to the airport."

"Sounds good. Talk to you later."

Anthony hung up the phone. He took a deep breath. Lori looked at him affectionately.

"What?"

"You! I haven't seen you like this in quite a long time."

"Like what?"

Lori walked up to Anthony. "I don't know – you seem to have a hop in your step. You seem more excited than I can remember."

"I'm just trying to make sure everything goes alright."

"No, it's more than that. Even Kristy has noticed."

Anthony looked puzzled.

"Yesterday night Kristy told me that you seemed different. You're smiling more. You're talking more."

Anthony sat down. Lori sat next to him on the couch. "I could only imagine the emotions you're experiencing. I know you've been on such a roller coaster ride."

"I don't know. Maybe you're right. I mean, it wasn't so long ago that my father didn't exist. Now, he's coming to my house."

"Life is interesting, that's for sure."

"You're preaching to the choir. And the thing is, I want him to be proud of me. I want him to be proud of the life we've made here. Is that crazy?"

"Not necessarily."

"Sometimes I think I should still be angry at him. But then I want him to think highly of me. I really shouldn't care what he thinks. He probably hasn't earned that right. But it still matters to me."

"You know why? Because he's your dad. I don't think you're looking at him any longer as just your biological father."

"I think you're right."

"Kristy's right," she said. Lori gave him a kiss on his forehead.

CHAPTER 84

Boston's airport was busy. It's always busy. But it seemed more so today.

"When are they supposed to arrive, Dad?" Kristy asked.

"Let's see if it's still on time," Anthony responded, as he looked up at one of the monitors. "Looks like it's been pushed back a while. They're not supposed to arrive now until 6:15."

"Well, we have some time then," Lori noted. "Do you mind if Kristy and me go downstairs and check out some of the shops?"

"That's fine. I think I'm going to grab a cup of coffee."

"Ok. We'll be back a little later."

Anthony took a copy of the Boston Globe and sat at the counter of the coffee shop near the gate. He was reviewing the financial section when a man came up to him.

"This seat taken?"

"Oh, no, help yourself," Anthony said.

"Thank you, young man." The waitress asked the man what he wanted to order. "Just an ice water, ma'am."

The man looked over to Anthony. "So, what's new in the world today?"

"Hmm? Oh, I was just looking at the money section."

"Good news?"

"Looks like the markets are still up and down."

"Mmm-hmmm. Been that way for a while, huh?"

"Seems like you can never get ahead. "

"What goes up must come down."

Anthony chuckled. "Yeah, I guess you could say that. I wish it would stay up longer."

"I bet. I'm Jessop, by the way," the man said, as he held out his hand.

'Jessop? Were your parents mad when you were born?"

Jessop laughed heartily.

"I'm sorry, I really am. I'm just kidding you. It's just that I feel pretty good today. I'm Anthony. It's nice to meet you."

"Nice to meet you. Are you on vacation?"

"No, I live here."

"Oh, you mentioned you were feeling good. I thought maybe you were on vacation."

"No, I'm waiting for some family to come in."

"Ah, that's always exciting."

"Yeah, my father's never been to Boston."

"Have you lived here a long time?"

'I've been here for several years. It was my job that brought me here."

"But your dad never visited? Sorry, it's none of my business – don't mean to pry."

"My father and I were just reunited not too long ago."

"Really? Good for you. You must be excited today."

"I am excited - and nervous too."

"Mmmmm. You want to impress him?"

Anthony turned to Jessop. "Yes. I was trying to tell my wife, but I didn't know how to explain it."

"Well, I think it's natural. Children usually want to impress their parents."

"Yeah, when you're a kid."

"Oh, I don't think age has anything to do with it. Think about it. As long as we look up to our parents, and respect them, we want their approval. We may not need their approval, but we typically want it. We like it when they're proud of us, no matter how old we are. I think it's a way of validating.

"Well, I should be going, Anthony. It was really nice meeting you. I hope you enjoy the time with your dad. Embrace the moment. And, I'm sure he and Mary are very proud of you."

Anthony shook his hand. "Thank you. Best of luck to you in your travels."

Anthony turned and saw Lori and Kristy back at the gate. They heard the announcement that the flight had arrived. He joined them. They started getting their things together. Anthony stopped and looked back at the café.

"What's wrong, honey?" Lori asked.

"The gentleman I was talking to. I told him my father was coming in. We were talking, and he told me he was sure my dad and Mary were proud of me."

"Yeah, so?"

"I never mentioned my mother's name. In fact, my mother never came up in the conversation."

"You probably mentioned it while you were talking, and just didn't realize it. I do that all the time."

"No. I'm sure I didn't mention her name."

"Do-do-do-do-do…..oooh, spooky…"

"Stop. I'm being serious. It's just strange. Just like the guy at the rest area on Interstate 90."

"What? What rest stop?"

"Nothing. You'd probably just laugh at that too."

CHAPTER 85

"Here they are!" Kristy was really excited.

"Relax; it will be a while before they're off the plane."

"She's just excited, Anthony," Lori said.

After several minutes, Mary and James were helped up the ramp to the waiting area.

"Grandma!" Kristy ran up and gave Mary a big hug.

"Oh, honey, you're getting so big. Just look at you."

"Hello," Kristy said to James. She gave him a hug.

"Hello, Kristy, it's good to see you again. You're grandmother's right. You're even taller than the last time I saw you."

Anthony shook James hand, and gave Mary a hug. "How was your flight?"

"Not too bad, "James said.

"A little bumpy, I thought," Mary said.

Anthony looked at James. "Welcome to Boston, Massachusetts."

"I can't believe I'm finally here."

"We're going to take you on a lot of sightseeing," Kristy noted.

"Easy, Kristy. Let's give them a chance to get acclimated and unwind."

"Oh, we're okay," Mary said to Anthony. "We are definitely looking forward to seeing the city, Kristy. I know what Mr. Evans can't wait to see."

"You bet – Fenway Park. I just want to touch the outside brick, and say that I was at Fenway."

"Well, we'll get you there, for sure," reaffirmed Anthony.

It took a while for everyone to get settled into Anthony's van, but eventually they left Logan.

"Wow, look at that," Mary said, as she pointed toward the harbor.

Lori looked at James' face. She could tell there was a sense of astonishment. He looked like a little kid on Christmas morning.

"We'll take you down to Quincy Market. You'll love the seafood. A lot of great shops, too," Anthony said.

"Do you like seafood, Mr. Evans?" Lori asked.

"Boy, I used to eat it a lot many years ago."

"Anthony's right – you won't find better seafood than up here."

"Well, then I'll have to give it a try."

They drove for a while. Anthony started to slow down. "So, you're excited to see Fenway Park?" he asked James.

"You know it!"

"Well, look to your left."

James looked over. "Ok."

"You're looking at Fenway."

"You're kidding. It doesn't even look like a stadium from the outside."

"A lot of people say that. I think it's because when most people think of stadiums, they envision the newer ones."

"It's the oldest ball park. I'd rather see this park than the newer stadiums."

"Don't worry. We'll take you down here during the day."

Mary looked at Lori. They smiled. They knew exactly what each other was thinking.

CHAPTER 86

"Your yard looks great," Mary told Lori. They were sitting on the back deck.

"Thank you. Can't take too much credit for it, though. Anthony does most of the landscaping."

"He always liked working outside. Everything has to be just perfect."

Lori chuckled. "You don't have to tell me that. You know, Kristy has a lot of that. She frustrates me sometimes. Everything has to be just so. Two peas in a pod, those two."

"Speaking of Kristy, where is she?"

"She's putting a puzzle together with Mr. Evans."

"Oh, God, you know I didn't know how things would go. But he seems to be fitting right in."

"I had a feeling everything would work out."

"You had faith in everything, Lori. That's such a good virtue. I sometimes wish Anthony had a stronger faith – a stronger belief in things."

"Oh, you know he's always been so practical. But I'll say this – I've been seeing some little changes in him."

"Tell me."

"I don't know. Lately he just seems a little more open. A little more introspective."

"Well, I'm sure the surgery had a lot to do with that. Don't they say that physical changes can cause people to experience emotional changes?"

"I guess. But I think there's more to it. I think it's almost spiritual."

"Spiritual? You're kidding."

"I didn't mean to alarm you. It's not like he signed up to be a member of the parish council at the local church."

Mary laughed out loud.

"No, I mean he has always been so focused and driven. Not that he isn't still driven. But, he seems to be taking a step back, and dare I say, even gaining some perspective. Even Kristy has noticed it."

"Maybe he's just starting to appreciate things more."

"Well, whatever it is, I have to admit, it's been nice."

CHAPTER 87

"Lori, you awake?"

She looked at the alarm. "Jesus, Anthony, it's 5:30."

"I know. But we have to get my mom and James ready."

"It's not going to take five hours for them to get ready. Go back to sleep."

"Hmmmm."

She turned her back to him, and laid on her other side. She smiled.

Anthony went downstairs and made a fresh pot of coffee. He took his cup and newspaper and sat on the back deck. It was quiet. Peaceful. It was early but he could tell it was going to be a hot one. He sat and watched the sun come up.

Mary opened the back screen door. "Sorry, didn't mean to startle you."

"You didn't. Where's your cane?"

"And a Happy 4th of July to you!"

He smiled. "Sorry. Happy 4th." He got up and gave Mary a kiss.

"I feel really good this morning. I was able to walk without any help."

"Just as well – I wish you would use your cane."

"Are you afraid I might fall and sue you?"

'Hahahaha. That's cute."

"Lori was right."

"What's that?"

"Oh, nothing."

'Lori was right about what?"

"There has been something different about you."

"Oh, not you too."

"I meant it as a compliment."

Anthony went inside and brought a cup of coffee for Mary.

"Thank you." She took a sip. 'Ooh, that's good. Do you sit out here often?"

"Actually, no. At least I never used to. I was always too busy."

"And now?"

"Well, since the surgery I've had to slow down a lot."

"Lori said you started back at work part time."

"Yeah, I'm lucky my bosses have let me ease back into things."

"They sure seem like good people."

"They are. But, I know this ain't going to last forever. Eventually I'll have to get back full time, and things will get back to normal."

"They don't have to."

"Oh, yes it does. Business is business. I'm going to have to work my ass off to gain some new clients. I'm not looking forward to that."

"Hmmmm."

"What?"

"Oh, I remember a time when getting the next sale was the most important thing to you."

"It's still important. But, I have to admit – it's been nice spending more time with Lori and Kristy."

"That's good to hear."

"So tell me about you and James. How are things going?"

"Pretty good. We are spending more time together. We talk about the past a lot. Sometimes it saddens me."

"Thinking about what could have been for you two?"

"Yes. But it also saddens me when I think what could have been for him. Anthony, I wish you could have seen him when we were kids."

"He was something, huh?"

"He really had the whole world ahead of him. He was handsome, athletic. And he was smart."

"I know he was recruited to play college football. Did he ever tell you why he didn't go to college?"

"He really hasn't said too much about that. Of course he joined the Army instead. Boy, he was such an intelligent young man. He was going to design buildings. He was interested in architecture and engineering. Back then, millionaires were very few and far between. Not like today. I really thought he was going to end up very wealthy."

"I imagine he lives with a lot of regrets."

"I think deep down, he does. But he really doesn't talk much about it. We seem to end up talking about my life instead. I figure when he's ready, he'll talk."

"Well, we can't do anything about the past. But we can give him a day to remember."

Mary smiled. "I don't know what some of his past Fourth of July 4's were like, but I have a feeling this could be his best ever."

CHAPTER 88

"Good morning," James said, as he made his way outside. Anthony helped him through the door.

"Thank you."

"We thought you'd sleep in," Mary said.

"Too excited to sleep. What's on tap for today?"

Anthony and Mary looked at each other and smiled. He had no idea.

"Let's get you a cup of coffee," Anthony said.

"That sounds great. Wow, what a great view. He has a lot of space back here."

"Anthony said some people bought the land back there and are supposed to start building soon – past that tree on the right."

"Oh, he's gonna have some neighbors."

"Yeah, I told him he could always put up a privacy fence. He told me I was being a bit presumptuous."

"They might end up being good neighbors. You never know," James said, trying to be the optimist.

Anthony brought out a new pot of coffee. "Thank you. And Happy 4th, by the way."

"Happy 4th."

"You looking forward to a big day?" Anthony asked.

"Sure am."

"Well, we'd like to hit some of the sights later this morning. Then, we're going to have dinner back here later."

"You'll hear no argument from me. Looks like it's going to be a really nice day."

"I think it might end up being a perfect day," Anthony said slyly.

CHAPTER 89

"We got everyone?" Anthony asked.

"Think we're ready," Lori said. "We're good to go."

"I hear Jennifer and Jacquie upstairs. Are they coming?" James asked.

"No, they're going to stay back and make dinner."

Kristy helped Mary and James get into the van.

Anthony headed out towards Fenway Park.

"This is the way to Fenway?" James asked.

"Sure is."

"Do you think we would have time to take a few pictures outside of the Park? Just a few pictures, is all."

Anthony looked at the others. "I think we'll have a few minutes."

"Great."

As they got closer to the stadium, James got more excited. He sat up in his seat. "They're playing the Blue Jays today. Should be a good game. The Jays always play them tough. Boy, they sure have a great day to play baseball."

They drove around the outside of the stadium. Anthony parked. He got out and slid open the passenger side door. Two security guards came up to the van.

"Mr. Evans?" one of the guards asked.

"Ah, yes, I'm James Evans."

"It must be your birthday," the guard responded.

"No, it's not my birthday."

"That's just an expression," Kristy was quick to respond. "It means this must be your lucky day."

"My lucky day?"

Everyone got out of the car. A gentleman in a sport shirt came out to greet them. He approached Anthony.

"Good morning. Are you Anthony?"

They shook hands. "I'm Brent Harris. I'm with the Red Sox staff."

"Nice meeting you."

"And you must be Mary and James. It's nice meeting you."

"Thank you, young man. It's my first time at Fenway."

"That's what I hear. We're glad to have you. We have some surprises for you."

"Well, one of my dreams has already come true. I'm sitting here in front of Fenway."

Anthony took Brent aside. "Thanks very much for having us," Anthony said. "He has no idea he's actually going to be watching the game."

"It's our pleasure. Chuck Parsons set this up. He wanted to make sure James was taken care of."

"Chuck's my boss. I know he has a lot of connections to the team."

"Oh, yeah. He's been a huge supporter of the Sox."

"I know that. The Sox are always a main topic of conversation in the office."

"Well, like I said we have some surprises. How about we get everybody inside?"

Anthony approached James. "How would you like to see the Sox play today?"

"You're kidding!"

"No kidding. We're going in."

James' face lit up. He was speechless.

They went inside. The smell of hot dogs and sausage was overwhelming. Some of the players were stretching in the outfield. The grounds crew was spraying water around the infield dirt.

A security guard approached them. "Would you like to take a tour of the stadium?"

"Yeah, let's do that," Kristy said excitedly.

With that, James not only got his first look at Fenway from the outside, but was going to get an intimate view inside.

After the tour, they were led to their seats. Front row along the first base line. They were very close to the Red Sox dugout.

James sat back, and tried to take it all in. He had seen this place dozens of times on TV. Now, he was actually here. It was surreal. He wanted to enjoy every moment.

A couple of official-looking people came over.

"Anthony?"

"I'm Gene Sorensen. We're ready."

"Great." Anthony looked over to James. "How's your pitching arm?"

James looked puzzled. "Come on – you're going to throw out the first pitch."

"You're shittin?"

"No shittin."

Mary, Lori and Kristy had no idea this was in store. As the security guard opened up the wall and assisted James, Lori took hold of Anthony's arm.

"Sorry, maybe next time you can throw out the first pitch," Anthony said to Lori.

Lori batted him with her other arm. "It's not that. I'm just curious how you were able to pull this off."

"Well, one of the executives at work mentioned the kidney transplant to a couple members of the Sox staff when they were at a golf outing. They found out we were coming to Fenway today, and set it up so that James could throw out the first pitch."

"You too, sir," the guard said to Anthony. "You're going to throw out the first pitch with your dad."

"Are you serious? I hope I don't make an ass of myself,"

"Don't worry," Lori said. "Only 37,000 people are watching."

"Thanks for the encouragement. "

From the press box, they announced James and Anthony and provided a brief background regarding the kidney transplant. They received a big round of applause.

They posed for a few pictures, and then Gene gave them each a baseball. James would throw first. For an old guy it wasn't a bad throw. Anthony followed up with a nice toss of his own.

They received another round of applause.

The catcher walked up to James and Anthony. He took off his mask and handed the baseballs to them. "Congratulations gentlemen."

"Thank you," Anthony said. He gave him a long look. The catcher seemed somewhat older. He certainly wasn't on the Red Sox roster.

"How are you feeling?" the gentleman asked James.

"I'm feeling pretty good – like I'm getting a little stronger every day."

"That's great. Remember, you're never too old to learn – never too old to grow. It's all about helping others. You guys are living proof of that. Well, take care of each other."

With that, he walked away. James and Anthony looked at each other.

"You know, he kind of reminds me of someone," Anthony said.

"I know what you mean. I feel like I've talked to him before."

Anthony turned to one of the guards. "Excuse me; do you know who that gentleman is?"

"The catcher? I don't know anything about him. I guess he just started here. He goes by the name "J.C."

CHAPTER 90

After the last out, and a Red Sox victory, James sat and watched the players congratulate each other. By the seventh inning, clouds had started to roll in. It looked like rain was on its way, so the grounds crew was getting ready to put the tarp on the infield. Anthony and Lori thought it would be best if they waited until most of the crowd filed out before attempting to leave. James wasn't going to complain. This was the first time he was at Fenway, and at his age, he had to question realistically whether he would return. He wanted to look at every part of the field. He didn't want to miss anything.

Lori turned to James. "Well, what did you think?"

"It was sick. It was epic."

They all looked at James. "Where did you hear those terms?"

"I watch a lot of TV. Isn't that what you kids say when something is awesome – it's "sick"?"

Kristy was laughing. "You got it."

"This was a great day," James said to Anthony. "I can't thank you enough. Please thank your bosses for me."

"I'm glad you enjoyed it. I'm also glad the rain held off. I was worried about that."

"What a beautiful day," Lori added.

"It was perfect," James said somewhat quietly to himself. He looked out at the field one last time. It was time to leave.

CHAPTER 91

As they headed back to Anthony's house, everyone was quiet. Kristy and Mary had fallen asleep. James felt very relaxed. He enjoyed looking at the sights. This day couldn't get any more perfect. Or so he thought.

As they got near the house, thunder erupted. Mary and Kristy abruptly awoke. The skies opened. It was a torrential downpour.

Jennifer and Jacqui helped Mary and James get into the house.

"How'd it go?" Jennifer asked James.

"I had a great time. I had no idea I was going to see the game – let alone go on the field."

"It was tough keeping it a secret," Jacqui noted.

"I'm just so glad the rain held off," Mary said. "It's really coming down. Oh, well, good thing it's not snow."

"Speaking of snow," Jacqui said. "Come in to the living room."

They all went into the living room. "My God, what is all this?" Mary asked.

There was a large Christmas tree, decorated with red and green lights and old style ornaments. A star with an angel on it topped the tree.

There were Santas all over – many shapes and sizes. Garland and bright, white lights hung over the mantel.

"What is all this?" Mary asked.

"It's Christmas – in July," Lori said.

"When Jacqui and I looked at your letters, Jennifer noted, it was pretty apparent that you and Mr. Evans had dreams of spending Christmases together. We thought...well....why wait until December? You've waited long enough. Plus, we figured – how often are we going to be all together with Anthony living away? We wanted to take advantage of this opportunity."

Mary had tears in her eyes. She hugged her kids.

"What smells so delicious?" Mary asked.

"Cabbage rolls and mashed potatoes. Oh, and plenty of Christmas cookies," Jacqui said.

"That sounds wonderful," she noted. "What do you think, James?"

James put his hands over his stomach. Well, those ball park hot dogs and peanuts were filling, but I think I can handle some more."

"Why don't you all take a seat in the dining room," Jennifer said. "Everything will be ready in a few minutes."

Kristy was under the tree, looking at the presents.

"What? You think there's something under there for you?" her mom asked. "Get over here and let's eat."

They gathered at the table. "Can I say something?" James asked. "I wanted to thank everyone for everything you've done for me. A year ago, I was just a man waiting to die. Anthony, you said a while ago that part of your healing process was that I gave you life. Well, you gave me a new life – not just physically, but you gave me a new reason to live – family. It's been so many years, that I forgot what family feels like. You've all given my life new meaning. I don't know if I believed in fate, but right now I do think Mary and I were meant to reunite. And, I think it was God's plan that I would find my son. I'm just very thankful to be here."

"I propose a toast," Anthony said. "To our family – and to fate."

They toasted, and ate a delicious meal together. Jennifer and Jacqui told of funny stories when they were kids. They laughed. They shed tears. It would have been a perfect end to a perfect day. But it wasn't over yet.

"Let's go open the presents," Jennifer said.

"Presents?" Mary asked.

"You didn't notice them when you came in?"

"My gosh, I didn't even see them. I don't have any gifts for anyone."

"You're not supposed to. This was a surprise, remember?"

They gathered around the tree. The rain was coming down very hard. It was already dark. The temperature had dropped. With the Christmas lights on it had the feel of Christmas Eve night.

Kristy opened a couple gifts – summer outfits. She was looking at two Christmases that year, so anything was a bonus.

Jacqui pulled a couple gifts from under the tree. She gave one each to Mary and James. "Jennifer and I hope you don't mind, but after discovering your letters we wanted to do something special."

They opened up their gifts together. Inside were necklaces. Each had two hearts hanging from it. The words inscribed on

Mary's were "My Jimmy, Second Chances." On James were the words "My Mary, Second Chances."

"I think it's beautiful," Mary said.

"I agree," James said. "The words say it all."

"I really like the two heart sets," Mary added.

Jacqui laughed. "Yeah, part of the reason for two hearts was because of all the lettering. But the first heart reflects what you two exchanged as kids. The second heart represents this new time in your life."

Jennifer and Jacqui hugged Mary. It was a very emotional moment.

Anthony spoke up. "I also have a present for you, Mom. It's not under the tree. It's not something you can unwrap. Lori, it's also for you. It's something I had been thinking about for a while. "

Lori seemed genuinely confused. "Well, what is it?"

"In August I will be starting catechism classes at St. Paul's. I plan to be baptized."

"Cool," Kristy replied.

"Wow. Are you sure you?" Lori asked.

"Anthony, I hope this isn't because of me," Mary said. "I hope you are not doing this because you feel pressured."

"Not at all. I have been meeting with Father Rice. I feel like I'm ready."

"Well, then I'm very happy for you...and very proud of you," Mary noted.

Anthony quickly thought back to what Jessop told him – that no matter what your age we always like to impress our parents. We want them to be proud of us.

"Ditto that," Jacqui said. "Jennifer and I have noticed some changes in you the past few months.

"You're right, Jennifer," James said. "Someone once told me – in fact it was today - that you're never too old to learn, or to grow."

"This has been such a wonderful day. I don't know how it could get any better," Mary noted. "James, do you remember when we were kids, and we would dream about spending Christmas together?"

"I sure do. And here I am. I found you, family, and I finally found Christmas."

Anthony chimed in. "And I think maybe, I have finally found the true meaning of Christ."

CHAPTER 92

Later that evening, after the rain had finally stopped, they all sat on the back porch. It was about 10:00. In the distance they could see the start of fireworks over the harbor. Mary and James looked at each other and laughed. They remembered where they were the first time they saw fireworks together.

"What are you guys laughing about?" Lori asked.

"Oh, nothing, honey...nothing at all," Mary replied. Some things were better left unsaid.

Our family celebrated Christmas twice that year. On Christmas Eve, we all got together at Jennifer's house. We had a great time. It snowed so hard we all ended up staying overnight. And, that night, my mom and dad did something I never thought I would see – they went sled riding together in Jennifer's back yard. We all tried to stay up as long as we could. We continued to stoke the fire in the fireplace, and drank hot chocolate and eggnog.

The following year, on July 4th, James and Mary were married. They were married by Pastor Rice – the same pastor who baptized my dad. The ceremony was held outside, near Rosemont's beautiful gardens. They moved into one of the housing units on the Rosemont campus. It had the feel of an actual house...and home.

We were fortunate to be able to celebrate several more Christmases. James actually got up to Boston a couple more times, and saw a couple more games at Fenway Park.

Almost 12 years after the kidney transplant surgery, James caught an infection he just could not fight. He died with Mary and my dad at his side. He had a necklace on when he passed. It had two and a half hearts on it.

James and Mary became so close, they were inseparable. Although they were not married very long, they seemed to make every moment count. They were given a second chance, and they made the most of it.

When James passed a large piece of Mary also died. She died just a year later. They said she died of natural causes. I think she died of a broken heart.

My dad was promoted to management at his firm. Over time, he successfully learned how to balance work and family. He was always good at his job. But, he became a greater father. His faith and spirituality remained an integral aspect of his life.

They say everyone gets a second chance in life. You just have to be able to recognize it. Fortunately, James and Mary did. And they weren't the only ones. My dad was given a second chance to gain perspective, forgiveness, and most of all, love. Because of that, my parents' marriage was given a second chance. They continued to grow closer and continue to enjoy learning more about each other. Sounds like they had a great example to follow.

I miss James and Mary very much, but will forever have their memories in my heart. They helped make me the person I am today. I was recently married, and I just hope I can be as good a wife and mother as Mary and my mom.

Today I am employed at a large company in Boston. I work as an architect, with a specialty in commercial building design. I just finished designs for an addition to a hospital that will be utilized primarily for transplant operations.

Kristy

My Dearest Mary –

By the time you read this I will have already passed on to the next life.

I don't want you to be sad. I am so grateful that I was given a second chance – that we were given a second chance.

We may not have had a "middle", but we had a beginning and an end. And those were the best times of my life.

They often talk about a person's first love as if it's something that should be bottled and stored away. As if it is something that's a phase in a person's life that has no effect on the rest of their life. But no matter what happened in my life, my feelings for you never changed. There was always a place for you in my heart. When we reunited, I learned how to open up the rest of my heart. Remember when I told you that Titanic was my favorite movie of all time? I loved everything about the story, but the real reason is that Jack and Rose reminded me of us. Regardless of what happened in Rose' life, you could sense that she never lost those feelings for her first love – Jack. She carried that through her entire life. That's what I have done with my feelings for you.

These past years with you were wonderful. It's what I had imagined when we were just kids. I've enjoyed talking to you, sharing with you, crying with you, laughing with you, and dreaming with you. You and Anthony taught me that no one is too old to dream…and that dreams definitely come true.

When we met so young, I quickly realized just how beautiful you were --- inside and out. You remain that way today. You are the most caring and giving person I have ever met. I do believe God created an angel when he created you.

I have also come to believe that God works through angels and people in everyday life. I've come to learn that He doesn't give us the answers to everything – he gives us the faith and grace, and the free will, to seek the answers and to do the right thing.

I certainly wish I could have watched our son grow up. I am so sorry that I missed that very important part in your life...and his. Everybody will go through life with regrets, and I certainly regret that every day. But it was Anthony who actually showed us how to forgive, and how to make the rest of our time on earth count. When we were so young, you told me so many times that you would give me a son, and he would play football, and make me proud. The fact is, I could not have been more proud of our son. He didn't have to play a sport. He did something so much more important – he sacrificed, he believed, and he saved my life. To paraphrase Rose in "Titanic," you and Anthony ended up saving my life in every way a person could be saved.

Don't be sad. I know we will meet again on the other side. We will all meet again. And, we'll be reunited once more.

I love you – I always have.

Your "Jimmy"

P.S. When we were young kids, you always said I was full of surprises. Well, here's one more. Do you remember when we had a picnic at the Lake? I had brought out my acoustic guitar and played you a song that I wrote you? I had kept that song all these years. I had never finished it. I want to make sure I finish what I started. So, here it is:

"Somewhere in the future,
She's waiting there for me.
All I want is a chance at love,
A chance for her to see."

"If fate holds on tight,
And the angels hear my prayer.
We'll be together soon, my love,
We have a bond that's just so rare."

"I love you more and more each day, you see,
You make my whole life complete, you and me.
I love you more and more each day, you see,
You make my whole life complete, you and me."

"She changed my life, she filled my world,
She saw deep into my soul.
She opened my eyes to a brand new love,
When I'm with her, I lose control."

"I love you more and more each day, you see,
You make my whole life complete, you and me.
I love you more and more each day, you see,
You make my whole life complete, you and me."

"Forgive me now, my faults are many,
I wish I was stronger.
But I never stopped thinking of you, my love,
My love is forever longer."

"My life has come full circle now,
That was impossible without you.
Every day is a blessing from God,
Everything is a gift brand new."

"I love you more and more each day, you see,
You make my whole life complete, you and me.
I love you more and more each day, you see,
You make my whole life complete, you and me."

"As I say good-bye, tears fill my eyes,
I just wish I had more time.
But nothing can replace the memories we made,
I just thank God you were mine."

EPILOGUE - ONE MORE SURPRISE

Shortly after James and Mary were married, Anthony had one more major surprise for James' birthday. Anthony, Lori and Kristy were on vacation for a week, and had visited Mary and James.

"Surprise!"

James just about jumped out of his skin. He and Mary had just returned from the flea market.

"Holy cow, you scared me."

"Happy birthday, Dad," Lori said.

"Thank you." He looked over to Mary. "Did you have something to do with this?"

"No. Honest. I didn't know a thing."

A couple of their closest friends from Rosemont were there in James and Mary's garage. Anthony allowed about 10 minutes for everyone to get situated. He then brought out the biggest surprise.

"Dad, Mom -there's something in the kitchen. We have another surprise for you." Anthony whistled loudly. "Ok, guys, come on out."

From the kitchen entered Lenny Parks, Jerry Sullivan and Stevie Johns.

"Oh my God," Mary said, as she held her hands over her mouth.

It didn't hit James at first. Until he saw Stevie come out last. He hadn't changed much. His dark hair was thinner, but he still wore it a little longer in back.

"Oh my God is right!" He went up to the guys and hugged each of them. They hugged and kissed Mary. Mary had tears running down her cheeks.

Lenny was bald. He was tall and slender. He looked in great shape for his age. He had spent a career in the Marines. He retired early. He and his wife, Frances, had four children.

Jerry couldn't stop smiling. Same old Jerry. Same easygoing demeanor he had as a kid. He enjoyed life. He had a pretty big gut on him. He obviously did not miss any meals. He was wearing a fishing hat, much like he did in high school. He ended up meeting another gentleman in the beer industry. They became business partners, and together they opened a number of beer distributors. He has lived in Indiana for several years. His wife, Eileen, died of breast cancer about five years ago.

And then there was Stevie. He still had a thin built, although he had a little bit of a beer gut. He was wearing old jeans. He was divorced a long time ago. He and his girlfriend, Janice, live together. They still lived in the area. He had worked at several car dealerships, as a mechanic. About ten years earlier he had purchased a service station.

They put their chairs in a circle. They talked about their youth.

"Do you remember the drag race?" James asked. "Boy, we worked on Stevie's car – making sure we got that thing ready. It definitely wasn't street legal."

Everyone laughed. "Yeah, as I recall, Hoss, I was the only one who got busted." James smiled. He felt good that Stevie still called him "Hoss."

"Yeah, I just happened to get pulled over by a cop who was a West Cannon alumnus."

Mary interjected. "No, the police officer's brother had played football for West Cannon."

"Oh, that's right. Damn, we were lucky."

Lenny spoke up. He looked at Anthony. "That's what we loved about your dad. He was a heck of a football player, but he didn't just hang around with the other players on the team. He never alienated us. Your dad made sure we always hung around together."

"I just had a lot of fun with our group, and with the "Hearts," James noted.

"Oh, yea, the "Hearts." Did you ever stay in touch with them, Mary?" Lenny asked.

"Well, for a couple years after high school, some of us stayed in touch. Joanie Sestak's parents were very strict. They did not like the idea that Joanie was still friends with me after they found out I was pregnant. They thought I might be a bad influence. Rhonda Sue, Barbara and I still hung around for a while." Mary paused. "But, things change, you know. And we lost touch."

"Rhonda Sue had moved away for a while," Stevie chimed in.

"Yeah, didn't she get married and live in Philadelphia?"

"Yep. But, after her divorce she moved back here."

Stevie had his arms folded around his chest. He had his legs stretched out. He was leaning back in his chair. "One time she had dropped off her car at a dealership I was working at. We made some small talk. I think she was embarrassed, actually. She had trouble holding on to jobs. I think she and her second husband were separated at the time."

There was a silence for about ten seconds.

"Anybody need a refill?" Anthony asked.

"Oh, I'll take another, sir," Jerry said, still smiling. "Thank you."

"I'll take another," Stevie noted. They could tell Stevie's love of beer never wavered.

"So, you spent your career in the military?" James asked Lenny. "We were kind of shocked when you enlisted at the end of high school."

Lenny was sitting straight up. "Well, my intention was to serve for a couple years, and then maybe go to college later. But, I re-enlisted and ended up spending many years there."

"And your family's doing well?" Mary asked.

"Yes, the kids are going great. Two are doctors, one's an attorney, and my youngest is a pharmacist. We have six grandchildren."

"Wow, good for you," Mary stated.

"Jerry, I see you're still a fisherman at heart," James said.

Jerry laughed. He spoke slowly. "Oh, yeah, I try to go fishing four or five times a week. I also hunt. I just enjoy the outdoors."

"We are so sorry to hear about your wife," Mary said.

"Well, thank you. I appreciate that. She didn't suffer long. Cancer took her quick." He paused. "Sure gets lonely. But I try to keep busy."

Again, there was silence for a short time. That is, until Stevie stirred things up. "Hey, do you remember Catherine?"

Mary poked him in the arm. "You had to mention her."

Everyone was laughing.

"Hoss, I apologize now. I don't think I helped the situation then," Stevie said with a grin.

"If I recall, Stevie, you thought it was quite humorous."

"That I did. God, she was a pain the ass, wasn't she?"

"This was the girl you told me about, Mom?" Jennifer asked.

"The one and only. She almost caused us to break up," Mary said as she looked at James.

"Stevie, I'll never forget the advice you gave me that night at the dance. You told me that I shouldn't deal with problems - I should eliminate them. That was the night I said enough was enough."

"I said that?"

"You did. You always gave me advice. Maybe not always great advice, but you were always there for me."

Stevie smiled.

"So enough about us. How have you been feeling, Jim?" Lenny asked.

"I'm feeling pretty good. No major problems. I feel a lot better than I used to."

"That's great to hear. Anthony, you're doing okay, as well?"

Anthony was seated at the table behind them, munching on some Doritos. "Yes. I feel good. So far, so good."

"How about you guys? Any major health concerns?" James asked.

The guys looked at each other. Lenny spoke up first. "I've been pretty fortunate. I've slowed down some. But, I haven't had any major health problems."

"I had a slight heart attack some years back," Jerry noted. "They put a stent in. I am feeling okay. I still eat what I want."

"We can tell," Stevie said, as he gently slapped Jerry's stomach. Jerry let out a hearty laugh.

"What about you, Stevie?" Mary asked. "Everything okay?"

"Yeah, I guess. Just old age. I did have problems with my pancreas. The doctor said I needed to cut way back on the drinking. I did...for about a month. I felt worse when I wasn't drinking, though."

"You still enjoy sports?" Lenny asked James.

"Yeah. We have a satellite dish, so I watch the Red Sox games. I try to watch as much college and pro football when I can. I still enjoy it." James paused. "But, to be honest I feel ashamed or guilty sometimes when I'm watching football."

"Why?"

James leaned back in his chair and started rubbing his hands through his hair. "Oh, sometimes I'll think back. I had a chance to play college football. I gave that up. It still puts a bad taste in my mouth."

"You were young, Jim. Things don't work out like we want."

"Here, here," Mary said.

Lenny continued. "You ended up with something much more important. You discovered your family, and you have a new lease on life. It's absolutely amazing what you and Anthony have been through, with the transplant."

"Thank you," James and Anthony said in unison.

"Hey, how about we sing Happy Birthday to the birthday boy, and cut some of this delicious cake," Jacqui said.

"That sounds like a plan," Jerry said. "I am hungry for some cake!"

They guys looked at each other, and laughed. Leave it to good ole' Jerry. Keeping things simple.

After cake, the guys went into the house and played several hands of poker at the dining room table. They ate and drank. They laughed. They recalled funny stories from their youth. They may have been old, but they were wise. They took Anthony to task, and showed him a thing or two about poker.

They stayed overnight. The next day, Stevie left. James and Anthony took Lenny and Jerry to the airport to catch their flights.

It was very sad to see them go. On the way back to James's house, James thought about when he and the guys drove home the last day of high school. Today had that same kind of feeling. He knew this was a once in a lifetime weekend. And he knew he would never see them again.

"Thank you, son. Thank you for everything," James said as he looked at Anthony.

"No problem. I am glad they were able to make it. It was a great weekend."

"It sure was."

"I could tell you guys have a bond that was never broken."

"Yeah, I guess you're right. Sounds like a couple other people I know..."

Anthony looked at James, and smiled. He recalled his talk with Peter Jansen. Peter was right. Anthony and his dad were forever connected in a very special way.

Made in the USA
Lexington, KY
06 December 2013